Meals in a Jar

Quick and Easy, Just-Add-Water, Homemade Recipes

Julie Languille

T0321295

ULYSSES PRESS

To Larry, my sweet husband, and Alex, Kaylah, and soon-to-be Matt,
thank you for letting me follow my heart, and your help and patience along the way.

Published by:
Ulysses Press
PO Box 3440
Berkeley, CA 94703
www.ulyssespress.com

ISBN: 978-1-61243-163-5
Library of Congress Catalog Number: 2013930886

Printed in the United States

20 19 18 17 16 15 14 13 12

Acquisitions Editor: Kelly Reed
Managing Editor: Claire Chun
Editor: Lauren Harrison
Proofreader: Elyce Berrigan-Dunlop
Editorial Associate: Lindsay Tamura
Design and layout: what!design @ whatweb.com
Illustrations: © Melanie Mikecz
Cover photographs: © Kim Nelson

IMPORTANT NOTE TO READERS: Trademarks of businesses and food brands mentioned in this book are used for informational purposes only. No sponsorship or endorsement by, or affiliation with, the trademark owners is claimed or suggested by the author or publisher.

Table of Contents

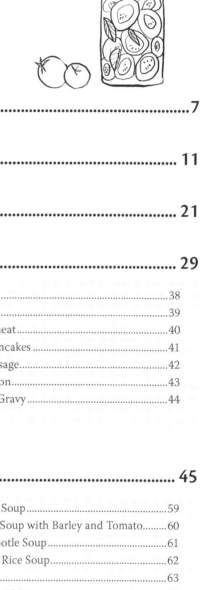

Chapter 6
Primarily Pasta.. **71**

Chapter 7
Ready-Made Main Course **85**

Chapter 8
Ready-Made Meals Sidekits **119**

Chapter 9
Snacks, Beverages, and Extras **143**

Chapter 10
Desserts **153**

Chapter 11
Logistics **169**

Recipe Index **173**

Acknowledgments and About the Author **175**

Chapter 1

Ready-Made Meals

I love walking into a full pantry, lined with neatly arranged shelves of food in jars and boxes all stacked in rows. Better than a candy store to me, the shelves of baking supplies, canned goods, and my own home-canned meats and vegetables all please me greatly, but what I like best are my own "ready-made meals." I have bags, jars, and boxes of shelf-stable meals, which I consider to be my own treasure trove and insurance against hardship or hunger. From the convenience of weeknight hustle to the moderate or dramatic circumstances of disaster, my store of shelf-stable meals means I am ready to feed my family well quickly and easily, with a minimum of fuss or effort and no trip to the grocery store for extra ingredients.

I have designed a whole variety of complete meal kits, packaged sets of everything you need to make a meal for your family—just add water. They can be packaged in Mason jars, in bags with handles to easily grab and go, or sealed into plastic bags. I have a variety of each, and this book will show you how to put together a food kit for seven days of food for your whole family, stored in complete meal kits in plastic tubs or lined up neatly in your pantry.

What Is a Ready-Made Meal?

A ready-made meal is a jar or bag with everything you need to create a complete meal with no additional ingredients except water. Ready-made meals can be breakfasts, lunches, dinners, snacks, breads, and desserts. There are options for how you store them, and you can choose what works best for your family and unique situation.

Ready-made meals come in three varieties: pressure-canned complete meals, dry meals, and meals that are a combination of the two and are packaged together.

Dry Ready-Made Meals

Dry meals are those composed of dehydrated foods that just need rehydrating and heating. These meals can be stored in Mylar bags, vacuum bags, or Mason jars and last longer if vacuum-packed and stored with an oxygen absorber. Dry meals can last for decades when stored in a cool, dry, dark location. Ingredients for dry meals include pasta, rice, beans, spices, freeze-dried meats, and other dry dehydrated or powdered ingredients. Dry ready-made meals include soups and bean dishes.

Pressure-Canned Ready-Made Meals

Pressure-canned meals are those that contain any meats, liquids, or anything other than completely dry ingredients. They may be pressure canned in pint- or quart-size canning jars, or in retort pouches, which are special metalized plastic bags designed to withstand the heat and pressure of pressure canning and have been approved by the FDA as safe for heat processing food. Some brands of tuna now sell products that have been canned in retort packages, so you can see samples of retort packaging on the shelf at your local grocery store.

Combined Ready-Made Meals

Combined ready-made meals include both canned and dry components that are packaged together to easily grab and go. Examples of combined meals are pasta and meat sauce, where the sauce is made and canned together with the meat, and the pasta is measured out and packaged with it to make a complete meal. Other examples include chicken canned with vegetables, which could be packaged with noodles to make chicken soup, packaged with flour and pie crust makings to be a chicken pot pie kit, or many other recipes such as a chicken-noodle bake, chicken and rice, or chicken and biscuits.

Why Ready-Made Meals?

Taste

It would be so easy to just buy pre-fab freeze-dried entrees and MREs for my family, but commercially prepared, pre-packaged food simply doesn't taste as good as what we can make with wholesome ingredients. I know we can make better-tasting food that our families actually want to eat that is satisfying, nourishing, and tasty.

Quality

Commercially prepared foods often contain ingredients that were grown with pesticides and chemicals and packaged with preservatives, artificial flavoring, and artificial colorings. Ready-made meals can be made with organic ingredients and locally grown meats and produce. You can even use food you grow yourself to make your own shelf-stable ready-made meals.

Convenience

At the end of another hectic workday, I gaze into my pantry and ponder the daily question of what to make for dinner. I have a few types of frozen meat (aka, protein icebergs) in the freezer I could thaw, mix with other things, and make into some form of meal, or I could mix up a pasta or casserole from the ingredients on the shelf, but you know what really beckons me? It's the easy-to-cook, all-ready-to-go, shelf-stable meals. Nothing beats the convenience of having ready-made meals to heat up or do some minor assembly for and knowing I have a sure-fire winner that my family will love, and no further effort or thinking is required from me. Score!

Preparedness

Filling my pantry with ready-made meals is, to me, the ultimate form of preparedness for my family. Whether faced with short-term unemployment, the occasional power outage during a storm, or a variety of other disasters, or even just a trip to the forest or lake for an impromptu camping trip, having food on the shelves that I can grab, prepare with a minimum of fuss, and nourish and hearten my family means peace of mind for me.

I am also of the mind-set that we should also be prepared for longer-term challenges, for disruptions in the power grid, or "the end of the world as we know it." My family always hopes and prays for the best but prepares for the worst, knowing that if hard times happen, we will be able to not just survive, but thrive, and be able to help others if we can.

Cost-Efficiency

Rising prices are a constant of everyday life. Packaging your food ahead in volume allows you to leverage bulk prices, discount stores, warehouse club stores, food co-ops, and membership buying clubs. You can package up to a year's worth of chicken or beef in a day and assemble several varieties of meal kits from them for the very lowest prices available.

Grab and Go

Another great feature of ready-made meals is their portability. Great for camping or emergencies, simply grab a box or two or twelve and be on your way. Many of us live where an earthquake, tsunami, fire, or flooding could cause us to need to leave our homes in a hurry. Why not plan ahead for that and have a box of food ready to go?

Great Gifts

It is always a blessing to take someone a meal. After the birth of a child, an illness, or a surgery nothing could be more cheering than a warm, filling, delicious meal. With a ready-made meal you can easily share a dish either hot and ready to serve or packaged to keep on their shelf to save for another time.

Chapter 2

Canning and Dehydrating

Canning Safety

There are two types of canning: water bath canning and pressure canning. Both types require careful attention to safety rules and must be done when you have the time and attention to ensure you are following all the guidelines. If not done properly, canned food can lead to food poisoning.

The ultimate authority on food-canning safety is the USDA, which does constant research into home-canning safety and occasionally updates its recommendations. It is critically important to follow the most recent guidelines from the USDA. All canning recommendations are current as of the time of this writing, but cannot be kept current thereafter. Be sure to verify current USDA guidelines before attempting any canning procedure.

Water Bath Canning

Water bath canning can be used to preserve high-acid foods such as fruits and tomatoes. For water bath canning, food is stored in sterilized jars, topped with warmed lids and rings, and then boiled for a specified period of time.

Water bath canning is great for making jams and jellies and preserving spaghetti sauce (without meat) and salsas. It cannot be used for meats or other non-acidic foods, so for the majority of this book we will be focused on using pressure canning to put up the protein portions of our ready-made meals, but canned fruit does make wonderful snacks, desserts, and side dishes. Most foods that can be water bath canned may also be canned in a pressure canner. Foods can be either raw packed (placed in the jar in a raw state) or hot packed, which means the food is heated to a simmer and cooked for two to five minutes before it's canned. Please refer to the chart below for details and always refer to USDA guidelines for their latest recommendations.

Water Bath Canning Processing Times (in minutes to process)				
Food	Style of Pack	Jar Size	Water Bath Canner	Pressure Canner
Apples, sliced	Hot	Pint	20	8
		Quart	20	8
Applesauce	Hot	Pint	15	8
		Quart	20	10
Berries	Hot	Pint	15	8
		Quart	15	8
Berries	Raw	Pint	15	8
		Quart	20	10
Cherries	Hot	Pint	15	8
		Quart	20	10

Water Bath Canning Processing Times
(in minutes to process)

Food	Style of Pack	Jar Size	Water Bath Canner	Pressure Canner
Cherries	Raw	Pint	25	10
		Quart	25	10
Fruit Juices	Hot	Pint	5	Not recommended
		Quart	5	Not recommended
		Half-gallon	10	Not recommended
Peaches	Hot	Pint	20	10
		Quart	25	10
Pears	Hot	Pint	20	10
		Quart	25	10
Plums	Hot or Raw	Pint	20	10
		Quart	25	10
Tomato Juice or Vegetable/Tomato Blend	Hot	Pint	35	20 (5 PSI) 15 (10 PSI) 10 (15 PSI)
		Quart	40	20 (5 PSI) 15 (10 PSI) 10 (15 PSI)
Tomatoes, crushed	Hot	Pint	35	20 (5 PSI) 15 (10 PSI) 10 (15 PSI)
		Quart	45	20 (5 PSI) 15 (10 PSI) 10 (15 PSI)
Tomato Juice	Hot	Pint	85	40 (5 PSI) 25 (10 PSI) 15 (15 PSI)
		Quart	85	40 (5 PSI) 25 (10 PSI) 15 (15 PSI)
Tomato Sauce	Hot	Pint	35	20 (5 PSI) 15 (10 PSI) 10 (15 PSI)
		Quart	40	20 (5 PSI) 15 (10 PSI) 10 (15 PSI)

Pressure Canning

Pressure canning is used to preserve low-acid foods such as meats, beans, and vegetables and is used in this book to create shelf-stable components of meals for everything except recipes that only contain dry ingredients.

There are some limitations in the USDA guidelines for home canning that are specific as to what ingredients can and cannot be used. Current guidelines instruct not using flour, pasta, rice, or other thickeners in any pressure-canned meals, or canning pureed dense vegetables.

An alternative to flours, starches, and other thickeners is clear jel, a modified cornstarch that withstands the heat and pressure of pressure canning. Clear jel can be purchased online, and, like cornstarch, thickens liquid into a transparent, gelatinlike consistency. Clear jel is used in some of the recipes in this book, but where gravy is required for a recipe, I prefer to make fresh gravy using the classic method of fat and flour cooked together with stocks or broths to create a rich, velvety sauce. The gravy is made after the food is removed from the jar or canning pouch.

Although small pressure canners can cost less than $100, they can also be quite expensive, costing several hundred dollars. I highly suggest you buy the biggest one you can afford as it will make it possible for you to process big batches of food, which will save time and money.

Pressure Canning Using Retort Pouches

Retort pouches only recently became available to the home canner. Similar to Mylar bags or "metalized" bags, retort pouches are specially formulated for pressure canning food. It is important to use retort pouches and not Mylar bags for pressure canning because retort pouches are made of material that has been approved by the FDA to hold food and to be heated under pressure. Other plastic materials may not be safe.

Similar to the pouches in which you can now buy some brands of tuna at the grocery store, retort pouches are lightweight, flexible cans that are not easily breakable. Unlike glass jars used for generations for canning, retort pouches can easily withstand an earthquake or even a fall from a pantry shelf without breaking. Retort pouches are great to put in a bug-out bag, an emergency kit with seventy-two hours of survival supplies in case you need to leave your home quickly. Retort pouches are also relatively inexpensive, but they are not reusable; once opened, they must be thrown away.

Retort pouches come in two styles: flat pouches, like the commercially packaged tuna pouches, and gusseted stand-up pouches, which are my preference. Flat pouches must be laid nearly flat to seal, and any liquid has a tendency to come forward, potentially hampering the seal. Gusseted pouches can be sealed in an upright position either using a jaw-style impulse sealer or by holding the pouch up to a vacuum-sealer and manually triggering it to only seal, and thereby not vacuuming the liquid contents up out of the pouch.

It is very important to leave plenty of headspace when canning with retort pouches or the pressure may cause the seals to come open during processing.

Flat retort packages are often used by fishermen to preserve their catch. The packages are heavily touted on the internet by sellers of very expensive "chamber" style vacuum-sealers. Chamber sealers are built to allow the food and bag to be placed inside a chamber. The air is then vacuumed out of the chamber. Since the pressure both inside and outside of the bag remains equal, the fluid in the bag is not suctioned out of the bag, which could result in a mess and/or a failed seal due to the presence of moisture during the sealing process. Chamber sealers are very expensive, with home models starting in the $700 range and continuing upwards of $3000.

Both cost and convenience factor into my preference for gusseted-style retort packages. I use the vacuum-sealer I already owned to seal my pouches. (Be sure to process a test batch of one or two bags before canning a whole batch of protein to be sure that a) your seals are strong enough for this size bag, and b) you've left enough headspace.) If you don't have a vacuum-sealer, you may be easily able to use an iron. You must be able to hold or place your food about 8 inches below a heatproof surface and then be able to bend the plastic up and over to be ironed closed. You need about a ½-inch seam or more.

If you are not successful sealing your bags with a vacuum-sealer or iron, or if you prefer an easier solution, jaw-style impulse sealers are available for retort bags for about $150. Simply fill upright bags and close the tops together with your fingers, pressing out as much air as easily possible, and then clamp on the jaws of the sealer. Note: As the gusseted bags are filled, the gusseted portion expands, gains weight, and becomes functional for making the bag stand upright. This part of the operation is easier with two people, one to support the bag until it become self-standing and one to ladle the liquid. Alternatively, you can use an empty, washed-out can, such as a spaghetti sauce can, to hold the bag while filling. Fold the top edge down over the rim of the can to keep it out of the way when filling and use a canning ladle.

Just as with Mylar bags and glass canning jars, it is important to keep the sealing surface clean and dry from food and liquid to ensure a good seal. Use a canning funnel to fill your pouches and if there is some spillage, wipe the area dry with a paper towel before sealing. If your mixture contains fats or oil, moisten the paper towel with a bit of vinegar before wiping to clean the fat from the area to be sealed.

Pressure Canning Instructions

Pressure canning requires the ability to read and follow directions well. Failure to do so could threaten your family's health. Please follow all directions carefully and follow current USDA guidelines for proper timing and procedures.

When pressure canning, choose from the allowable sized jars, and determine whether the food can be canned raw or must be hot packed after cooking until two-thirds done. Place the food in sterile jars, leaving the required amount of headspace (headspace is 1 inch for vegetables and all meats except chicken and rabbit, which is 1½ inches). Alternatively, food can be placed in retort pouches and sealed with 1½ inches of headspace. Note: Headspace is especially important if using retort pouches, because too little headspace will cause the bag seams to fail.

Wipe the top rims of the jars clean. Place the lids and rims on and tighten them by hand. Heat a few inches (about 1 gallon) of water in your pressure canner until hot and steaming. Add the jars or retort pouches one at a time on the racks so the jars are not sitting on the bottom of the canner.

Close the canner according to manufacturer's directions. Heat the canner until it begins to steadily vent steam. Set a timer for ten minutes and wait for the ten minutes to elapse, which will give time for the air to be vented from the canner.

Place the correct weight on top of the canner, wait for it to come up to the prescribed pressure, and begin timing according to the given times for the food you are canning and the size jar you are using.

After the time has elapsed, turn the heat off and allow the canner to cool. Once cool enough to touch, remove the jars or pouches to a towel on the counter and allow to cool completely. Once cooled completely, check the seals by pressing on the lids. Well-sealed lids will not spring back after lightly pressed. Poorly sealed lids will pop down and back up. If properly sealed, the jars may be stored. Refrigerate any unsuccessfully sealed jars and use quickly.

The information in the charts below was current only at the time of writing and current best practices may have subsequently changed. Please follow current USDA recommendations.

Pressure Canning Processing Times—Vegetables (in minutes to process)			
Vegetables	Raw or Hot	Pints	Quarts
Asparagus, spears or pieces	Either	30	40
Beans or peas, shelled, dried	Hot	75	90
Beans, baked or dry, with tomato or molasses sauce	Hot	65	75
Beans, fresh lima, shelled	Either	40	50
Beans, snap and Italian, pieces	Either	20	25
Beets, whole, cubed, or sliced	Hot	25	30
Carrots, sliced or diced	Either	25	30
Corn, cream-style	Hot	85	No
Corn, whole kernel	Either	55	85
Mixed vegetables	Hot	75	90
Mushrooms, whole or sliced, hot pack (½ pint same as 1 pint) Note: Wild mushrooms cannot be canned safely.	Hot	45	No
Peas, green or English, shelled	Either	40	40
Peppers (½ pint same as 1 pint)	Hot	35	No
Potatoes, sweet, pieces or whole	Hot	65	90
Potatoes, white, cubed, or whole	Hot	35	40
Pumpkin and winter squash, cubed	Hot	55	90
Spinach and other greens	Hot	70	90
Succotash	Hot	60	85

Pressure Canning Processing Times—Meat (in minutes to process)			
Proteins	Hot or Raw	Pints	Quarts
Chicken or rabbit, cut up, without bones	Either	70	90
Chicken or rabbit, cut up, with bones	Either	65	75
Ground meat	Hot	75	90
Chopped meat	Either	75	90
Strips, cubes, or chunks of meat	Either	75	90
Meat stock (broth)	Hot	20	25
Fish	Raw	100	Not recommended
Smoked fish	--	110	Not recommended
Shrimp (cover in salted water)	Either	45	Not recommended

Pressure Canning Steps to Determine Time and Pressure

1 Determine whether to pack raw or if the food must be cooked through and hot.

2 Follow directions for headspace. (Headspace is 1 inch for vegetables and all meats except chicken and rabbit, which is 1½ inches.)

3 Determine processing time.

4 Determine pressure based on elevation for either a dial-gauge or weighted-gauge pressure canner.

   a. Dial-Gauge Canner:

Altitude	Pressure
Sea level–2000 feet	11
2000–4000 feet	12
4000–6000 feet	13
6000–8000 feet	14

   b. Weighted-Gauge Canner: Use 15 pounds for all

Dehydrating Food

Dehydrating food is really easy and very satisfying. Almost every fruit or vegetable can be dehydrated. Most foods can just be washed, sliced, and dried. Really dense vegetables such as potatoes and sweet potatoes must be peeled and parcooked first. Simply spread out the food over the drying racks and dehydrate for six to twenty-four hours, depending on the food, until completely dry. Some drying times are listed below. For foods not listed, dry until the food is no longer sticky and it breaks rather than just bending when folded.

Vegetable Dehydrating Times			
Food	Preparation	Drying Time	Yield
Asparagus	Wash and cut into 1-inch pieces	5–6 hours	
Beets	Steam or bake until tender; cool, peel, and slice or dice	8–12 hours	
Broccoli	Wash and cut into florets	10–14 hours or until brittle	3 pounds (1 #10 can)
Cabbage	Wash, trim, and cut into ⅛-inch strips	7–11 hours	1 pound (1 #10 can)
Carrots	Wash, peel, and slice or dice	6–10 hours	
Celery	Dice	3–10 hours	15 pounds (1 #10 can)
Corn	Cook and remove from cob OR use frozen straight from the bag	12–15 hours	15 pounds (frozen) (1 #10 can)
Green beans	Wash, snap ends, and cut into 1-inch pieces	8–12 hours	
Onions	Slice or dice (do these outside due to odor)		
Mushrooms	Wipe clean, slice (wet mushrooms discolor)	10 hours or until brittle	5 pounds (1 #10 can)
Potato, diced	Cook, peel, dice		
Potato, shredded	Dehydrate straight from frozen		
Tomato powder	Wash tomatoes, slice, and crush in a blender once dried	12–15 hours	
Spinach	Wash, stem		1 pound (1 #10 can)

Fruit Dehydrating Times

Food	Preparation	Drying Time	Yield
Fruit leather	Cook and puree fruit, spread on plastic wrap over dehydrator tray	15–20 hours	
Apples	Peel, slice	12–15 hours	6.75 pounds (1 #10 can)
Blueberries	Wash and dry gently	18–20 hours	
Citrus	Slice paper thin	15–20 hours	5–6 lemons (1 #10 can)
Grapes	Wash	15–20 hours	
Nectarines	Peel, slice	12–15 hours	
Prunes	Whole	48 hours	
Peaches	Peel, slice	8–16 hours	
Pears	Peel, slice	12–15 hours	6.75 pounds (1 #10 can)
Plums	Peel, slice	12–15 hours	
Rhubarb	Slice	12–15 hours	

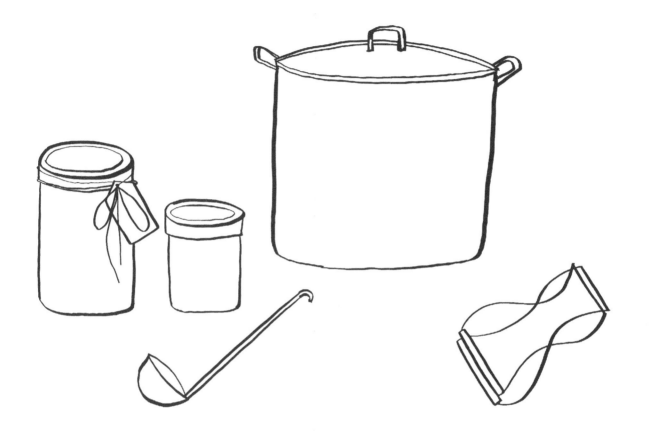

Chapter 3
Ingredients,
Equipment, Supplies

A Word about Ingredients

One of the things that sets ready-made meals apart from commercially available emergency foods is they are designed to taste really good. Although they're made using easily available ingredients, there are some ingredients that give a really big gain in flavor but which you might not find in everyone's kitchen. These can be easily bought online, or made at home from readily available ingredients.

Bouillon / Soup Base

Chicken, beef, or vegetable bouillon, bouillon cubes, or soup bases may all be used interchangeably in the recipes in this book. One teaspoon of bouillon mixed with 1 cup of water makes 1 cup of stock. Or, 2 teaspoons of bouillon plus 1 cup of water is the equivalent of a condensed or flavorful stock.

Cheese

Cheese is basically preserved milk, and it is relatively safe to eat for a lengthy period of time. There are several options for further preserving cheese by coating it in wax or vacuum-sealing chunks and storing it in a cool place, buying dehydrated cheese commercially, using processed cheese food such as Velveeta or Laughing Cow brands, relying on drier cheese such as Parmesan, or by water bath canning. When a recipe calls for cheese, plan to use your choice of home-canned, vacuum-packed, or processed cheese food.

Although I do not have long-term data available, I have water bath canned cheese and used it up to a year later with very good results. I grate the cheese, melt it, put it in wide-mouth half- or quarter-pint jars and process for thirty minutes. This changes the texture of the cheese, but it can be sliced or grated, tastes good on a cracker, and works well in cooking. I recommend starting with a mild cheese, because it becomes sharper with age. When I intend to use the cheese in Mexican or other spicy dishes, I add red pepper flakes before canning to give it some heat.

Washington State University makes and sells a natural (unprocessed) canned cheese called Cougar Gold, which keeps very well in cold root cellar temperatures. You can also dehydrate cheese and then grind it into cheese powder, or you can store cheese cubes covered in oil in sterilized canning jars. Please refer to current USDA guidelines for food preservation.

Processed cheese food such as Velveeta and Laughing Cow brand cheeses are also good shelf-stable choices.

For canned cheese:

4 pounds mild cheddar cheese

16 wide-mouth quarter-pint jars

Sterilize jars and lids and start a water-bath canner heating with water. Grate the cheese and heat in a pot over low to medium heat until melted. Divide the cheese among the jars and top each with ⅛ inch of oil from the melted cheese. Wipe the jar rims with a paper towel moistened with vinegar. Add jars to the water-bath canner, bring to a boil, and process thirty minutes. Remove and let cool completely. Wipe the jars clean.

Cheese can also be waxed or vacuum-sealed. This greatly extends the shelf life of cheese. To wax cheese, you must buy a specialized cheese wax, which can be found online or at cheese-making specialty shops.

Melt the wax and brush on three or four coats of wax to cover the cheese completely. To vacuum-seal cheese, cut it into 4-ounce cubes, place in small vacuum bags, and vacuum-seal.

Clear Jel

Clear jel is modified cornstarch that is able to withstand the heat of pressure canning. Clear jel may be added to foods before they are canned. It is available for purchase online.

Eggs

Some of the recipes in this book call for whole egg powder, which must be purchased. I know of no way to successfully dehydrate eggs at home because raw egg is perishable and would be subject to bacteria in the time it took to dehydrate. Commercial egg powder is freeze-dried, which makes the process safe. Egg powder mixed 1:2 with water reconstitutes into a product which is much like fresh, beaten eggs. Cans of whole egg powder are available online and at home stores like Walmart. Each can contains the equivalent of about 156 eggs. So although a can of egg powder costs more than fresh eggs, when you consider it contains thirteen dozen eggs, the price is actually much better. Powdered eggs will last about three years unopened; 1 tablespoon egg powder mixed with 2 tablespoons water is the equivalent of one egg.

Greens: Chard, Spinach, and Kale

Greens offer the most nutrition by weight of any food on the planet and are fabulous in soups or stews. You can add greens to ready-made meals if you dehydrate them first. Dehydrating greens couldn't be easier: Be sure to wash them well and blot dry with paper towels, then simply spread them over a dehydrator tray and dehydrate for six to nine hours. I like to grow my own in my garden, but you can watch for them to go on sale and buy a bunch, or purchase them in large quantities at a club or warehouse store. Once dried, vacuum-seal or dry-pack them (seal food in a metal can, typically a #10, if you have access to a can sealer), or keep them in resealable zip-top bags for packaging into ready-made meals. Dehydrated greens also make good snacks if you coat them lightly in olive oil before drying and season them well to add salt and flavor.

Milk

Dry milk is used in a variety of recipes as a substitution for fresh milk. Usually $\frac{1}{3}$ cup of dry milk stirred into 1 cup of water will produce 1 cup of milk.

Shortening / Oil / Butter

Recipes that call for cooking something in a small amount of fat will often call for a small amount of shortening to be wrapped in plastic wrap and included in the bag. Shortening has a very long shelf life, with estimates ranging from nine years to indefinite. If you prefer not to use shortening, you could substitute oil and either plan to have it on hand or tuck small bottles into your tubs of ready-made meals or you can use coconut oil or ghee. Whatever you choose, be sure to package or wrap it well so it doesn't melt out and over your dry ingredients. Many grocery stores carry tiny 2-ounce disposable containers intended for taking salad dressing in a lunch bag. These work well for fat or oil too. And if you don't care for the taste or fat profile of shortening, you can also substitute coconut oil, which is solid at room temperature, tastes delicious, and also has a long shelf life. It will melt on a warm day so be sure to package it well.

For baking with shortening, cooks have been using butter-flavored Crisco with great results for decades. Butter-flavored Crisco is available in cardboard cans and also packaged in 1-cup cubes. The cubes are quick and easy to measure and vacuum-seal.

Some recipes call for ghee, which is clarified butter. Often used in Indian cooking, ghee has delicious flavor, a very high smoke point, and keeps at room temperature for years. Ghee can be purchased commercially prepared, or home-canned into sterilized jars. The USDA has not yet published guidelines for home-canning ghee, but since the ghee is not truly canned (that is, it's not processed in either a water bath or pressure canner), they may never do so. Ghee has been prepared and used for generations in India.

To prepare ghee, sterilize quarter- and half-pint jars by boiling and then dry them. In a large pot, melt 2 to 4 pounds butter. Allow it to boil. It will boil rapidly at first and then slow its pace. Foam will float to the top, form a thick layer, clump into solids, and fall to the bottom. It will then foam in clearer bubbles, and at this point it is ready to package. Use a ladle to pass the liquid through layers of cheese cloth or a fine mesh strainer set on a canning funnel to filter the ghee and fill the prepared jars, leaving the solids behind in the pot. Leave 1 inch of headspace in each jar. Wipe the jar rims with vinegar-moistened paper towels. Let cool completely and then seal tightly.

You can allow your ghee to cook slightly longer to give it the deliciously nutty flavor of browned butter. You must watch it closely to ensure it doesn't become too brown and bitter.

Sour Cream Powder

Sour cream powder can be mixed with water (1 part water to 2 parts sour cream powder) to approximate fresh sour cream. Sour cream powder is delicious stirred into soups and paired with milk as a substitution for fresh cream in recipes.

Tomato Products

Diced tomatoes, tomato sauce, and tomato juice are so widely available in cans, it is simple to just buy them on sale at club or warehouse stores to add to your ready-made meals. If you do, please include a can opener in each of your tubs of weekly meals. Alternatively, if your garden, farm stand, or neighbor has gifted you with a glut of tomatoes, can those up for inclusion in your ready-made meals. Tomatoes keep beautifully in retort pouches for easiest portability, and also keep beautifully in classic, reusable canning jars. Pint jars are about equivalent to a 14.5-ounce can of store-bought tomatoes, although they hold about 16 ounces and, a 1-quart jar would stand in for a 28-ounce can and hold about 32 ounces. You can also slice tomatoes, dry them in your dehydrator, and then crush them into tomato powder for use in recipes.

Powdered Vanilla

Powdered vanilla, or vanilla powder, adds amazing flavor to sweet things such as baked goods and pastries. Powdered vanilla can be a bit expensive, but you only use a tiny amount and it yields wonderful flavor. It will make the difference in your food, and your child's eyes will light up as they tell their sleepover guest, "Wait until you taste my mom's pancakes!" It will make your family love to eat your ready-made meals.

I buy powdered vanilla online at Amazon.com and choose the sustainably grown raw variety. There is a less-expensive kind available, intended to be added to lattes to add vanilla flavor without adding alcohol. If you choose this variety, you might like to increase the quantity you use. The raw ground beans are a stronger concentration and require only a tiny pinch in each bag. If using the other powdered vanilla, you might use ¼ teaspoon per 4-serving bag.

Equipment

Vacuum-Sealer / Jaw-Clamp Sealer

A bag sealer is a must-have. Ideally you need one that will seal vacuum bags and retort pouches and will also have an attachment to vacuum-seal canning jars. You can often find vacuum-sealers at thrift stores and garage sales. If they have the tiny round port, they will likely accept the vacuum tube with the can-vacuuming attachment. I use a Weston 2300, which unfortunately doesn't come with that attachment, but it does seal retort pouches and is a champ with vacuum bags. Be sure to test a single retort pouch in the pressure canner sealed with your vacuum-sealer to ensure the seams will hold before you seal a whole batch of food to can. If the seams of your test pouch don't hold, increase the headspace and/or widen your seal.

You can also seal retort pouches with a "jaw" clamp-style sealer, which is available online. You can also use a household iron to seal retort pouches and Mylar bags.

Dehydrator

Dehydrators can also be purchased at thrift stores and garage sales. If you decide to buy a new one, I prefer the Excalibur, which is widely believed to be best. If you already have one, or buy one used, make a note of where the fan is. If it is at the bottom of the unit, you'll need to dehydrate a single food at a time to avoid mixing flavors and scents. With the Excalibur, the fan is at the rear so you can vary the ingredients in the trays without blending scents and flavors. With all types of dehydrators, spread the food to be dried, and use a low temperature (120°F or less) and rotate your trays at least once, halfway through.

Water Filter / Bottled Water

Ready-made meals do require water. If your circumstances might make water scarce, consider packing bottled water in your meal kits. In my area of the country, it rains quite regularly, and if filtered and boiled, the rainwater easily becomes potable. My family keeps a Berkey water filter for just this purpose. We also catch rainwater from the roof and store it in a tank. In case of drought, there are many lakes near us. But if you live in an arid climate, plan to have your own water available for both cooking and drinking.

Roaster Oven

A roaster oven is a tabletop appliance that makes it possible to cook large quantities of food at once using moist heat, also called braising. Roaster ovens come in sizes from 5 or 6 quarts all the way up to an 18-quart capacity to accommodate a very large turkey. Roaster ovens are wonderful for cooking large, inexpensive cuts of meat and poultry, and the long, slow cooking time transforms even the toughest cuts into tender, flavorful deliciousness.

Rocket Stove

I always want to be prepared to cook in a disaster or no-power situation, and I like to use a rocket stove. A rocket stove will burn twigs and sticks and creates a very hot fire quickly with readily available fuel. You can make a rocket stove from cans, or buy one. I use one made by StoveTec (www.stovetec.net).

Solar Oven

Solar ovens are great for cooking any time you have sunshine and they can be left to cook unattended. They can reach temperatures upward of 300°F depending on the available sunlight. Not to state the obvious, but they do stop working once the sun goes down, so if a solar oven is your main cooking appliance, you might choose to serve your big meal earlier in the day and plan a lighter meal at night when your oven likely won't be working. Good solar ovens include the Global Sun Oven (www.sunoven .com) and my favorite, the Sport (www.solarovens.org).

Wonder Oven

A wonder oven is an insulating device that insulates a hot pot of food so well that the retained heat will finish the cooking. A wonder oven looks a bit like a bean bag chair, only smaller, cube shaped, and with a lid. It is actually filled with polystyrene balls, just like a bean bag chair. To use a wonder oven, heat a pot to boiling on another stove or fire, or rocket stove, and then nestle your hot pot and lid into the wonder oven to finish cooking over the rest of the day. It works like a no-electricity-needed slow cooker, using retained heat to slowly cook your food over several hours. Plan for food to cook for about twice as long as in a traditional slow cooker. You will get delicious results without having to attend to the food, and it is easier to hide from the dog, because you can cook with the stove inside on a table or counter. The best wonder ovens are made by my friend Angie Jerome at Eco Wonder Oven (ecowonderoven.com). You can also make one yourself if you have the patience to deal with polystyrene balls. Patterns are available online.

Supplies

Vacuum Bags

Vacuum-sealer bags can be bought online or even at Walmart. Good vacuum bags are at least 3 millimeters thick. Consider also getting some rolls of vacuum material so you can create bags of any size. Many of the meals in this book require smaller packets of ingredients like dry milk. Vacuum bags are great, except for fragile foods, such as some types of pasta, which would be crushed during sealing.

Canning Jars

Canning jars can be bought everywhere from the grocery stores and your local hardware store to thrift stores and garage sales. If you buy used jars, be sure to check the opening of the jar, skip any with chips on the edges, and plan to buy new lids and rings for them.

Retort Pouches

Retort pouches are specialized bags that can be used for pressure canning in lieu of glass jars. They are lightweight and shatterproof, although they can be punctured. Retort pouches can be purchased online. They come in 1-quart, gusseted pouches, but can be cut to a smaller size if desired.

Mylar Bags

Mylar bags are very lightweight, but tough and very durable—a perfect solution for sealing together several components of a ready-made meal. Mylar bags don't stack well, so consider storing filled Mylar bags in plastic bins or buckets. This also adds another layer of protection against rodents and other pests. Rodents have been known to chew through some incredibly dense materials.

Grocery Bags and Totes

I use paper tote bags from the grocery store for packaging some of my meal kits. They are free in the produce section (look near the potatoes or apples) and I can keep a steady supply of them if I remember to grab a few while I am grocery shopping. Also, if you ask the bagger to use plastic, not paper, bags when you check out, you will get a pretty durable, lightweight, reusable bag perfect for storing a meal.

Chapter 4

Breakfast Is in the Bag

Omelet in a Bag

This is such an easy way to make eggs; even the kids can do it. You can add the water right into the baggie and mix in the bag, being careful not to poke a hole into the bag, or mix it in a bowl and then pour it back into the bag to cook.

Makes 16 (2 to 3-serving) meals

Ingredients

4 cups powdered eggs

1 cup finely grated Parmesan cheese (like Kraft brand)

¼ cup plus 2 tablespoons dried chives or thyme

4 teaspoons salt

2 teaspoons pepper

Ready-Made Meal Assembly

In each of 16 zip-top quart-size freezer bags, package:

- ¼ cup powdered eggs
- 1 tablespoon finely grated Parmesan cheese
- 1 teaspoon dried chives or thyme
- ¼ teaspoon salt
- 1 pinch pepper

Label each bag

Heat a medium pot of water over medium heat to just simmering. Add ⅓ cup of water to the bag and squish the bag to combine (or put in a bowl and stir with a fork). Place the bag of omelet mixture into the water and simmer 10 to 15 minutes, until solid and just cooked through. Divide the omelet into portions and serve. Serves 2 to 3.

Variations

Package this omelet alone, or pair it with a ½-pint of ham, bacon, or sausage. (Cooked sausage, diced ham, or bacon may be added to the omelet before cooking.) Or pair it with a Biscuit sidekit (page 126). This recipe can also be poured into a small baking dish lined with a pie crust (see Pie Crust Sidekit page 127) and baked into a quiche. Two omelet bags plus up to 4 cups of parcooked vegetables would make a full-size quiche, which could be made in a Pie Crust Sidekit or made crustless in a pie dish or an 8 x 8-inch pan sprayed with cooking spray.

2 Omelet kits (page 30) + 1 Biscuit sidekit (page 126) + ½ pint Ham/Bacon/Sausage = 8 breakfast sandwiches

2 Omelet kits (page 30) + 1 Pie Crust Sidekit (page 127) + 2 cups Vegetable Sidekit (pages 133–37) = 1 quiche

1 Omelet kit (page 30) + 1 Tortilla sidekit (pages 129–30) + 1 quarter-pint cheddar cheese = 4 breakfast burritos

Pancakes 4 Ways

The big flavor hit with these pancakes is the powdered vanilla. If your powdered vanilla is the vanilla-infused-sugar variety used in hot drinks, use about 1 teaspoon more per bag.

Makes 16 (4 to 6-serving) meals (about sixteen 4-inch pancakes each)

Ingredients

2 cups chopped walnuts or pecans (optional)

2 cups chocolate chips (optional)

2 cups dried blueberries, apples, or sweetened cranberries (optional)

20 cups flour (5 pounds)

7½ cups dry milk

3¾ cups sugar

3½ tablespoons salt

½ cup plus 2 tablespoons baking powder

1 cup vegetable shortening

8 cups syrup or 16 Syrup Sidekits (page 132), for serving (optional)

¼ cup plus 2 tablespoons powdered vanilla (optional)

Instructions

For optional additions: In each of 12 vacuum bags (4 bags will contain only pancake mix), add and then seal (or, use zip-top plastic bags and be sure to remove as much air as possible and seal):

- 4 (½-cup) bags chopped walnuts or pecans
- 4 (½-cup) bags chocolate chips
- 4 (½-cup) bags dried fruit

For pancake mix: In a very large bowl, whisk together the flour, dry milk, sugar, salt, and baking powder until very well combined.

For shortening: Wrap 16 (1-tablespoon) portions shortening each in a 4-inch square of plastic wrap.

For syrup, if using: In each of 16 (½-cup) mini round disposable containers (such as those made by Glad), package:

- ½ cup syrup

Ready-Made Meal Assembly

In each of 16 quart-size jars or vacuum bags, use a canning funnel to fill with:

- 2 cups pancake mix
- 2 teaspoons powdered vanilla (add on top)

Add:

- 1 packet shortening
- 1 container syrup or 1 Syrup Sidekit
- 1 package optional additions

Label each bag

Add 1 cup of water to dry ingredients and stir well until blended. Stir in the nuts, dried fruit, or chocolate chips, if included. Heat a skillet over medium-high heat and add some shortening. When melted and hot, add batter ¼ cup at a time and cook until fully bubbled and golden. Flip and cook until browned on the other side. Cook the remaining batter in batches, add more shortening as needed. Serve with syrup. Makes about 16 (4-inch) pancakes.

Wheat Berry Cereal

Super-nutritious and delicious. Be sure to use a good variety of your favorite fruits. You can use regular dried fruit or freeze-dried fruit, reconstituted at serving time with a little hot water.

Makes 16 (4-cup) bags (4 servings each)

Ingredients

6 cups dried fruit (raisins, blueberries, apples, or a combination)

2 cups granulated sugar or brown sugar

48 cups hard red wheat berries

Instructions

For fruit packets: Mix together the dried fruit and sugar. Measure ½ cup in each of 16 small vacuum bags, vacuum, and seal.

Ready-Made Meal Assembly

In each of 16 quart-size vacuum bags or jars, seal:

- 3 cups wheat berries
- 1 fruit packet

Label each bag

Soak the wheat berries overnight in 6 cups of water; or day of serving, combine the wheat berries and 6 cups of water in a pot, bring to a boil, reduce to simmer, and cook 1 hour. Divide into 4 bowls and top with fruit and sugar. Serves 4.

Muesli

Use your largest bowl to make this extra-large batch. If you don't have a bowl big enough, a food-grade, clean 5-gallon bucket or large plastic bag could work too.

Makes 16 (4-serving) bags

Ingredients

27 cups rolled oats

3 cups toasted wheat germ

3 cups wheat bran

3 cups oat bran

6 cups raisins, dried cranberries, or dried apples, or a combination

4½ cups chopped walnuts or pecans

1½ cups brown sugar

1½ cups raw sunflower seeds

4 cups dry milk

Instructions

For cereal: In a large bowl, combine all ingredients except milk.

For milk: In each of 16 vacuum bags, add and then seal:

• ¼ cup dry milk

Ready-Made Meal Assembly

In each of 16 Mylar bags, tote bags, or vacuum bags, store:

• 2 cups cereal   • 1 packet milk

Label each bag

Mix the dry milk with 2 cups of water and stir. Serve ½ cup milk with ½ cup cereal. Serves 4.

Morning Muffins 4 Ways

I think a hot, delicious, freshly baked muffin makes everyone feel special.

Makes 16 (12-muffin) batches, 4 packets each of 4 varieties: blueberry, cranberry, apple-cinnamon, and chocolate chip

Ingredients

32 cups flour

12 cups sugar

5⅓ cups dry milk

1 cup powdered eggs

4 teaspoons salt

10½ tablespoons baking powder

4 cups vegetable oil

4 cups dried apples

4 teaspoons ground cinnamon

4 cups dried blueberries

4 cups dried cranberries

4 cups chocolate chips

Instructions

For all muffins: In each of 16 vacuum bags or jars, add, mix, and then seal:

- 2 cups flour
- ¾ cup sugar
- ⅓ cup dry milk
- 1 tablespoon powdered eggs
- ¼ teaspoon salt
- 2 teaspoons baking powder

For oil: In each of 16 small vacuum bags or disposable 2-ounce containers, add and then seal:

- ¼ cup vegetable oil

For apple-cinnamon muffins: In each of 4 vacuum bags, add and then seal:

- 1 cup dried apples, chopped
- 1 teaspoon ground cinnamon

For blueberry muffins: In each of 4 vacuum bags, add and then seal:

- 1 cup dried blueberries

For cranberry muffins: In each of 4 vacuum bags, add and then seal:

- 1 cup dried cranberries

For chocolate chip muffins: In each of 4 vacuum bags, add and then seal:

- 1 cup chocolate chips

 Ready-Made Meal Assembly
In a vacuum bag, Mylar bag, or tote bag, package:

- 1 jar or pouch muffin mix
- 1 packet oil
- 1 packet fruit or chocolate

 Label each bag
Preheat the oven to 400°F. Grease a standard 12-cup muffin pan, or line with paper baking cups. In a mixing bowl, combine the muffin mix, oil, and 1 cup of water. Stir until well blended. Fill each prepared muffin cup only two-thirds full. Bake about 20 minutes, until muffins are lightly browned. Makes 12.

Cranberry Walnut Muffins

This combination of cranberries and nuts has a superbright flavor and is a great way to start the day. If you have raw sugar, package up enough to sprinkle on top before you bake the muffins. The crunchy sugar adds a wonderful texture contrast and crunchy burst of sweetness.

Makes 6 batches (18 to 24 muffins each)

Ingredients

15 cups flour

3 cups sugar

2 cups dry milk

¾ cup powdered eggs

6 tablespoons baking powder

2 tablespoons baking soda

3 teaspoons powdered vanilla

1½ teaspoons salt

4½ cups dried sweetened cranberries

4½ cups chopped walnuts or pecans

3 cups butter-flavored shortening or ghee

Instructions

For muffin mix: In each of 6 vacuum bags or jars, add and then seal:

- 2½ cups flour
- ½ cup sugar
- ⅓ cup dry milk
- 2 tablespoons powdered eggs
- 2½ teaspoons baking powder
- ½ teaspoon baking soda
- ½ teaspoon powdered vanilla
- ¼ teaspoon salt

For fruit and nut mix: In each of 6 vacuum bags, add and then seal:

- 1 cup dried sweetened cranberries
- 1 cup chopped walnuts or pecans

For shortening or ghee: In each of 6 vacuum bags, add and then seal:

- ½ cup butter-flavored shortening or 4 ounces ghee

 Ready-Made Meal Assembly

In each of 6 Mylar bags, tote bags, or vacuum bags, store:

- 1 jar or pouch muffin mix
- 1 packet fruit and nuts
- 1 packet shortening or ghee

 Label each bag

Preheat the oven to 375°F. Butter a standard 12-cup muffin tin or line with paper baking cups. In a large bowl, whisk together muffin mix and 1 cup plus 2 tablespoons of water. Stir until just combined (overstirring makes muffins tough) and add fruit and nut mixture. Fill each muffin cup three-fourths full. Bake about 25 minutes, until lightly golden. Makes 18 to 24.

Granola

This is a superdelicious granola. To make 16 bags at once, use a really big bowl and then toast it using your largest turkey-roasting pan. Stir frequently to get the toasty taste through and through.

Makes 16 (4-serving) meals

Ingredients

27 cups rolled oats

4½ cups wheat germ

4½ cups oat bran

3 heaping cups sunflower seeds

3 heaping cups finely chopped almonds

3 heaping cups finely chopped pecans

3 heaping cups finely chopped walnuts

1½ teaspoons salt

1¾ cups brown sugar

¾ cup maple syrup

2½ cups honey

3 cups vegetable oil

4 tablespoons ground cinnamon

4 tablespoons vanilla extract

6 cups raisins or sweetened dried cranberries

4 cups dry milk, packaged into 16 (¼-cup) packets

Instructions

For granola: Preheat the oven to 325°F. Line a large roasting pan or 2 rimmed baking sheets with foil. In a very large bowl or pan combine the oats, wheat germ, bran, sunflower seeds, and nuts. In a large saucepan over medium heat, heat together the salt, sugar, syrup, honey, oil, cinnamon, and vanilla. Pour over the cereal mixture and toss to coat. Spread in the prepared pan or on the prepared baking sheets and roast for 25 to 30 minutes, until golden and toasted, stirring periodically, or roast it in two batches on both baking sheets. Let cool completely.

 ### Ready-Made Meal Assembly
When the granola is completely cooled, in each of 16 vacuum bags, seal 2 cups of granola and a packet of dry milk.

Label each bag
To prepare, mix the dry milk with 2 cups of water and chill. Serve ¾ cup cereal and ½ cup milk per serving. Serves 4.

Breakfast Burritos

Burritos are the perfect grab-and-go breakfast: perfectly portable, and everybody loves them.

Makes 16 (4-serving) meals

Ingredients

4 cups powdered eggs

1 cup finely grated Parmesan cheese (like Kraft brand)

¼ cup plus 2 tablespoons dried chives or thyme

4 teaspoons salt

2 teaspoons pepper

2 pounds mild cheddar cheese

2 tablespoons plus 1 teaspoon red pepper flakes (optional)

16 Tortilla Sidekits (pages 129–30)

Instructions

For eggs: In each of 16 zip-top quart-size freezer bags, seal:

- ¼ cup powdered eggs
- 1 tablespoon finely grated Parmesan cheese
- 1 teaspoon dried chives or thyme
- ¼ teaspoon salt
- pinch of pepper

For cheese: In each of 16 wide-mouth quarter-pint jars, seal:

- 4 ounces mild cheddar cheese
- 1 teaspoon red pepper flakes

Or, cut 2 pounds cheese into 4-ounce cubes and wax.

 Ready-Made Meal Assembly
In each of 16 Mylar bags, tote bags, or vacuum bags, store:

- 1 bag eggs
- 1 Tortilla Sidekit
- 1 quarter-pint spicy cheese or 4 ounces waxed cheese

Label each bag
Heat a medium pot of water over medium heat to just simmering. Add ⅓ cup of water to the bag of eggs and squish the bag to combine (or put in a bowl and stir with a fork). Reseal the bag and place the bag of omelet mixture into the water and simmer 10 to 15 minutes, until solid and just cooked through. Divide the omelet into quarters, roll in the tortillas, add grated cheese, and serve.

Oatmeal

Homey and comforting as well as nutritious and fortifying, oatmeal is a great way to warm up a cold morning.

Makes 16 (4-serving) meals, 4 bags each of 4 varieties: apple, raisin, cranberry, and almond

Ingredients

32 cups quick-cooking oats

2⅔ cups dry milk

4 cups brown sugar

6 tablespoons ground cinnamon

1 cup raisins

1 cup dried apples

1 cup dried sweetened cranberries

1 cup chopped almonds

Ready-Made Meal Assembly

In each of 16 vacuum bags, add and seal:

- 2 cups quick-cooking oats
- 2 teaspoons dry milk
- 1 tablespoon brown sugar
- ¼ teaspoon ground cinnamon

- ¼ cup raisins, dried apples, dried sweetened cranberries, or chopped almonds

Label each bag

Bring 3 cups of water to a boil. Put bag contents into a bowl and then add boiling water. Stir, and then let sit 2 minutes, stir and serve. Serves 4.

Grits

I love grits. And polenta. Grits are typically made from white corn ground into coarse cornmeal and polenta is typically made with yellow cornmeal. Both are delicious and can be served either sweet or savory, particularly with cheese. Grits are usually paired with American or cheddar cheese, and polenta is usually paired with Parmesan cheese or mascarpone. If you want an alternative to using cheese, try grits topped with toasted nuts, brown sugar and/or toasted coconut. Yum.

Makes 16 (4-serving) meals

Ingredients

16 cups hominy grits

2 cups dry milk

3 tablespoons salt

1½ tablespoons freshly ground black pepper

4 pounds mild cheddar cheese, canned in quarter-pint jars or waxed 4-ounce chunks

Ready-Made Meal Assembly
In each of 16 vacuum bags, add and then seal:

- 1 cup hominy grits
- 2 tablespoons dry milk
- ½ teaspoon salt

- ¼ teaspoon freshly ground black pepper
- 1 quarter-pint mild cheddar cheese or 4 ounces waxed cheese

Label each bag
In a medium saucepan, bring 3 cups of water to a boil over high heat, add the dry grits ingredients and stir for 1 minute. Reduce the heat to low and cook, stirring frequently for 10 to 15 minutes, until no longer gritty. Meanwhile, grate the cheese. When the grits are done, stir in the cheese until melted, and serve. Serves 4.

Cream of Wheat

Doesn't Cream of Wheat just bring you back to your childhood? If you are eating from food storage, you can also grind your own Cream of Wheat by putting wheat berries through your food mill at a coarser grind than you would use for flour. You can find farina in the bulk foods section of the grocery store.

Makes 16 (4-serving) meals

Ingredients

30 cups hard red wheat, ground in your grain mill and measured out to be 42⅔ cups of ground wheat, or 42⅔ cups cream of boxed wheat cereal, or 42⅔ cups farina

4 cups sugar

2 tablespoons powdered vanilla

¼ cup salt

Ready-Made Meal Assembly
In each of 16 quart-size vacuum bags, add and then seal:

- 2⅔ cups ground wheat, cream of wheat, or farina
- ¼ cup sugar
- a pinch of powdered vanilla
- ¼ teaspoon salt

Label each bag
To prepare, combine 1⅓ cups of water with the dry mixture in a medium saucepan over medium heat. Simmer for about 10 minutes and serve. Serves 4.

Cornmeal Pancakes

Cornmeal pancakes have a lovely golden crust around the edges that makes a nice textural contrast between the crispy outside and the creamy, delicious inside.

Makes 16 (4-serving) bags or jars

Ingredients

22 cups cornmeal

2 cups brown sugar

½ cup salt

11 cups flour

1 cup baking powder

1 cup dry milk

2 cups powdered eggs

1 cup shortening

8 cups syrup or 16 Syrup Sidekits (page 132)

Instructions

For pancake mix: In a very large bowl, mix all of the dry ingredients together well.

For shortening: Wrap 16 (1-tablespoon) portions shortening each in a 4-inch square of plastic wrap.

For syrup: In each of 16 (½-cup) mini round disposable containers (such as those made by Glad), package:

- ½ cup syrup or 1 Syrup Sidekit

 **Ready-Made Meal Assembly**

In each of 16 quart-size vacuum bags or jars add, and then seal:

- 2½ cups pancake mix
- 1 packet shortening
- 1 packet syrup or 1 Syrup Sidekit

> **Label each bag**
> In a saucepan over high heat, bring 1⅔ cups of water to a boil, turn off heat, add dry ingredients, and stir until a smooth batter forms. Heat shortening in a skillet over medium-high heat. Pour batter ¼ cup at a time onto the hot skillet and cook until golden. Flip and continue cooking until brown. Serve with syrup. Makes about 12 pancakes.

Eggs and Sausage

This morning classic is always a welcome way to start the day.

Makes 16 (4-serving) meals

Ingredients

8 cups powdered eggs

2 tablespoons salt

1 tablespoon black pepper

1 cup shortening

8 pounds bulk breakfast sausage
or 8 cups freeze-dried sausage
crumbles

Instructions

For eggs: In each of 16 vacuum bags, add and then seal:

- ½ cup powdered eggs
- ½ teaspoon salt
- ¼ teaspoon black pepper

For shortening: Wrap 16 (1-tablespoon) portions shortening each in a 4-inch square of plastic wrap.

For sausage: If using fresh breakfast sausage, lightly brown the meat in a large skillet over medium-high heat . Using a canning funnel, fill 16 sterile ½-pint jars with cooked sausage or freeze-dried sausage crumbles. Wipe the jar rims clean with a vinegar-moistened paper towel. Top with heated lids and rings. Alternatively, seal the sausage in retort pouches. Pressure-can pints 75 minutes or as instructed by current USDA guidelines for your area.

 Ready-Made Meal Assembly

Seal or package together in each of 16 Mylar bags or tote bags:

- 1 bag egg mix
- 1 packet shortening
- ½ pint sausage

Label each bag
To prepare, mix the contents of the egg pouch with 1 cup of water. Drain the sausage (or if using freeze-dried sausage, soak in 1 cup of hot water for 10 minutes). Heat the shortening in a skillet over medium heat. Scramble the eggs and add the sausage, or heat separately and serve on the side. Serves 4.

Eggs and Bacon

Canning bacon is fun and surprisingly easy. You might like to crisp it further after you've opened it. Be sure to save any bacon drippings to add flavor to other meals.

Makes 16 (4-serving) meals

Ingredients

8 cups powdered eggs

2 tablespoons salt

1 tablespoon black pepper

1 cup shortening

8 pounds bacon

Instructions

For eggs: In each of 16 vacuum bags, add and then seal:

- ½ cup powdered eggs
- ½ teaspoon salt
- ¼ teaspoon black pepper

For shortening: Divide the shortening into 1-tablespoon portions and wrap each one well in plastic wrap.

For home-canned bacon: Arrange bacon in overlapping strips in parchment, roll up tightly, and insert into each of 16 wide-mouth pint-size canning jars. Wipe jar rims clean with a vinegar-moistened paper towel. Top with heated lids and rings. Alternatively, seal in retort pouches. Pressure-can pints for 75 minutes or as instructed by current USDA guidelines for your area.

 Ready-Made Meal Assembly

In each of 16 Mylar bags, tote bags, or vacuum bags, store:

- 1 bag egg mix
- 1 packet shortening
- 1 pint home-canned bacon

> **Label each bag**
> Mix the contents of the egg pouch with 1 cup of water. Cook the bacon in a skillet until crisp. Heat the shortening in a skillet over medium heat. Scramble the eggs and add the bacon, or serve on the side. Serves 4.

Biscuits and Gravy

Biscuits and gravy are a Sunday favorite at my house and seem like such a lovely, indulgent way to start off the day. Plus, they add some serious calories to fuel your family.

Makes 16 (4-serving) bags/jars

Ingredients

42¼ cups flour, divided

3½ cups shortening, divided

8¼ cups dry milk, divided

1½ tablespoons baking soda

⅓ cup baking powder

⅔ cup cream of tartar

⅓ cup salt

16 pounds bulk breakfast sausage, lightly browned and crumbled or 8 cups freeze-dried sausage crumbles

For gravy:

1 cup shortening, packaged in 16 bundles of 1 tablespoon each and wrapped in plastic wrap

1 cup flour, packaged in 16 bundles of 1 tablespoon each and wrapped in plastic wrap

1 cup dry milk packaged into 1 tablespoon packets wrapped securely in plastic wrap

Instructions

For biscuits: In a huge bowl, mix together 41¼ cups of the flour, 2½ cups of the shortening, 8¼ cups of the dry milk, and then baking soda, baking powder, cream of tartar, and salt. In each of 16 vacuum bags, add and then seal:

- 3 cups biscuit mix

Label each bag
Preheat the oven to 400°F. Mix the package contents with ⅔ cup of water. Pat into a round shape ½ inch thick and cut into biscuit-size rounds (or drop by spoonfuls) on a baking sheet and bake 10 to 12 minutes, until golden. Makes 12 large biscuits.

For shortening and flour: In each of 16 pieces of plastic wrap, combine and wrap well:

- 1 tablespoon shortening
- 1 tablespoon flour

For sausage: If using breakfast sausage, lightly brown the sausage in a pan and crumble. Using a canning funnel, fill 16 sterilized pint-size jars or retort pouches with cooked sausage and cover with water leaving 1 inch of headspace. Wipe the lids or rims to be sealed, add the lids and rims, or heat-seal the pouches. Pressure-can pints for 75 minutes or as instructed by current USDA guidelines for your area. If using freeze-dried sausage, vacuum-seal ½ cup in each of 8 bags.

Ready-Made Meal Assembly
In each of 16 Mylar bags, tote bags, or vacuum bags, store:

- 1 bag biscuit mix
- 1 packet shortening and flour
- 1 packet milk
- 1 pint sausage crumbles

Label each bag
Make the biscuits according to the directions. While the biscuits bake, heat the shortening and flour together in a skillet, stirring. Mix the dry milk with ½ cup of water. Add the milk to shortening-flour mixture, stirring. (If using freeze-dried sausage, add 1 cup of hot water to sausage crumbles and let sit 5 minutes and then drain.) Add water from sausage and stir until starting to thicken. Add sausage, stirring to break up. When thick, serve gravy spooned over biscuits. Serves 4.

Chapter 5

Soup's On

These soups can be stored in canning jars, which look very pretty and make nice gifts, or they can be sealed into Mylar bags. Vacuum-sealing makes them last longer and works with jars or bags, or you can use oxygen absorbers, small packets that can be added to containers to absorb oxygen (available online), which work equally well. If you fill Mylar bags so they can lay flat or stand upright in your pantry, soup storage is even more convenient.

If you choose to package these soups in a jar to give as a gift, be sure to add the ingredients in the order of the smallest ingredients first, so the largest ingredients are on top of the filled jar. For example, if a soup has large ingredients like beans, but also includes powdered ingredients like powdered soup base or spices, put the small powdered ingredients first and the larger beans on top. If the order is backward, the smaller ingredients will filter down and between the larger ingredients, and although the taste will be the same, the jars won't look as pretty and layered while sitting on the shelf.

An important variable in soup recipes is the powdered bouillon or soup base. Different brands of these ingredients vary in strength and saltiness, so I recommend making a single recipe of any given soup and adjusting the quantity used according to your taste before scaling up and making a large batch of several bags.

MEAT SUBSTITUTIONS: In recipes calling for meat, feel free to use either freeze-dried or home-canned meats such as beef, chicken, and sausage. Also, many of the beef soups are also delicious using sausage crumbles as well. Some cooks like to substitute textured vegetable protein (TVP) for all or part of the ground beef in recipes for the sake of economy. If using freeze-dried meats, use about half the amount called for, because it expands when it comes in contact with fluid. For example if a recipe calls for a pint of home-canned beef, you may substitute 1 to 2 cups of freeze-dried ground beef, beef chunks, or sausage crumbles.

Beef, Lentil, and Pasta Soup

This soup combines lentils, split peas, and barley, which are the quickest-cooking legumes, with tasty, tender home-canned beef. The legumes give a delicious toothsome chew and the tender beef and pasta make for a savory, nutritious, satisfying soup. Serve it with biscuits or cornbread.

Makes 8 (8-serving) meals

Ingredients

2 cups uncooked split peas

1⅓ cups beef bouillon granules

2 cups pearl barley

2 cups uncooked lentils

1 cup dehydrated onion flakes

3 tablespoons dried Italian seasoning

2 cups uncooked long-grain white rice

8 (½-pint) jars Home-Canned Beef (page 48) or 8 cups freeze-dried beef, sausage, or TVP

8 bay leaves

4 cups uncooked alphabet pasta

8 (14.5-ounce) cans diced tomatoes

8 (6-ounce) cans tomato paste

Instructions

For soup mix: In each of 8 vacuum bags or jars, add and then seal:

- ¼ cup uncooked split peas
- 2½ tablespoons beef bouillon granules
- ¼ cup pearl barley
- ¼ cup uncooked lentils
- 2 tablespoons dehydrated onion flakes
- 1 teaspoon dried Italian seasoning
- ¼ cup uncooked long-grain white rice
- 1 cup freeze-dried beef, sausage, or TVP (if not using home-canned beef)
- 1 bay leaf

For pasta: In each of 8 small zip-top bags, seal:

- ½ cup uncooked alphabet pasta (or other small pasta)

Ready-Made Meal Assembly

Seal or package together in each of 8 vacuum or tote bags:

- 1 bag soup mix
- 1 bag pasta
- 1 can diced tomatoes
- 1 can tomato paste
- 1 can home-canned beef (if using home-canned)

Label each bag

In a large pot over medium heat, add beef and any liquid and stir to break up. Add the diced tomatoes, tomato paste, soup mix, and 6 cups of water. Bring to a boil, and then reduce to simmer. Cover and cook for 45 minutes. Stir in the pasta, cover, and simmer 15 to 20 minutes, or until the pasta, peas, lentils, and barley are tender. Remove the bay leaf and serve. Serves 8.

Home-Canned Beef

Ingredients

4 pounds ground beef

seasoning salt

black pepper

8 (½-pint) jars

In a large skillet over medium-high heat, brown the beef and stir to break up. Season well. With a canning funnel, transfer into sterile jars, and cover with water, leaving 1 inch of headspace. Wipe jar rim with a vinegar-moistened paper towel. Pressure-can for 75 minutes. Let cool completely and wipe jars clean.

Cream of Asparagus Soup

This is a delicious, creamy, delicately flavored soup. The dehydrated asparagus really ups the flavor. Serve it with dinner rolls for dipping or a sidekit of Cheddar Garlic Biscuits (page 126).

Makes 8 (6-serving) meals

Ingredients

16 cups dehydrated asparagus

2 cups dehydrated chopped onion

2 cups dehydrated chopped celery

5 tablespoons plus 1 teaspoon garlic powder

2 tablespoons plus 2 teaspoons onion powder

1 cup chicken soup base or bouillon granules, divided

16 slices dehydrated lemon

1 cup dry milk

2 tablespoons sour cream powder

1 teaspoon ground nutmeg

1 cup butter-flavored vegetable shortening

1 cup flour

Instructions

For soup mix: In each of 8 vacuum bags or jars, add and then seal:

- 2 cups dehydrated asparagus
- ¼ cup dehydrated chopped onion
- ¼ cup dehydrated chopped celery
- 2 teaspoons garlic powder
- 1 teaspoon onion powder
- 1 tablespoon chicken soup base or bouillon granules
- 1 slice dehydrated lemon

For creamy mix: In to each of 8 vacuum bags or zip-top bags, add and then seal:

- 2 tablespoons dry milk
- 2 tablespoons sour cream powder
- 1 tablespoon chicken soup base or bouillon granules
- dash of ground nutmeg

For thickener: In each of 8 squares of plastic wrap, bundle:

- 2 tablespoons butter-flavored vegetable shortening
- 2 tablespoons flour

Ready-Made Meal Assembly

In each of 8 Mylar bags, tote bags, or vacuum bags, store:

- 1 vacuum bag soup mix
- 1 vacuum bag creamy mix
- 1 packet thickener

To package in a jar: Put the soup mix in the bottom of the jar, then the bag of creamy mix, then place the thickener packet on top.

Label each bag or jar

Combine the soup mix and 3 cups of water in a medium pot. Cook over low heat for 20 minutes or until asparagus is tender. Remove the lemon slice and turn off heat. In a small pot over medium-high heat, add the contents of the thickener packet and stir to melt and combine. Cook for 2 minutes, and then stir in the creamy mix powder and 1½ cups of water. Bring to a simmer, stirring constantly until thickened. Add the creamy mix to the asparagus mixture. Serve chunky or process through a food mill. Serves 6.

Black Bean Soup with Sour Cream

This is a very filling, full-flavored, stick-to-your-ribs soup. Make a sidekit of Corn Muffins (page 128) to go with it.

Makes 8 (8-serving) meals

Ingredients

8 cups dried black beans

4 cups dehydrated diced onion

2 cups dehydrated green pepper

4 cups dehydrated celery

4 cups dehydrated sliced carrots

5 tablespoons plus 1 teaspoon garlic powder

1 cup chicken soup base or bouillon granules

8 slices dehydrated lemon

8 teaspoons salt

4 teaspoons pepper

8 cups sour cream powder

Instructions

For soup mix: In each of 8 vacuum bags add, and then seal:

- 1 cup dried black beans packaged in a zip-top bag
- ½ cup dehydrated onion
- ¼ cup dehydrated green pepper
- ½ cup dehydrated celery
- ½ cup dehydrated sliced carrots
- 2 teaspoons garlic powder
- 2 tablespoons chicken soup base or bouillon granules
- 1 slice dehydrated lemon
- 1 teaspoon salt
- ½ teaspoon pepper

For sour cream: In each of 8 vacuum bags, add and then seal:

- 1 cup sour cream powder

Ready-Made Meal Assembly

In each of 8 Mylar bags, tote bags, or vacuum bags, store:

- 1 bag soup mix
- 1 bag sour cream

Label each bag

Soak the beans in water overnight or boil in water for 2 minutes and let sit for 2 hours. Drain. Add more water to cover by 2 inches and boil 90 minutes or until almost tender. Drain. Add remaining ingredients from the soup mix (not sour cream packet) and add 3 cups of water. Simmer 45 to 60 minutes, until beans are very tender. Remove from heat. Put sour cream powder in a small bowl and stir in ½ cup of water. Serve beans with a dollop of sour cream. Serves 8.

Cream of Broccoli Soup

This is my daughter's favorite soup—Kaylah loves broccoli. This recipe is easy enough for a tween to make and is just lovely served with some Cheddar Garlic Biscuits (page 126) or dinner rolls for dipping.

Makes 8 (8-serving) meals

Ingredients

2 cups chicken soup base or bouillon granules, divided

8 cups dehydrated onion

32 cups dehydrated broccoli

5⅓ cups dry milk

2⅔ cups sour cream powder

2 cups flour

2 teaspoons ground nutmeg

Instructions

For soup mix: In each of 8 vacuum bags or jars, add and then seal:

- 2 tablespoons chicken soup base or bouillon granules
- 1 cup dehydrated onion
- 4 cups dehydrated broccoli

For creamy mix: In 8 zip-top bags or vacuum bags, add and then seal:

- ⅔ cup dry milk
- ⅓ cup sour cream powder
- ¼ cup flour
- 2 tablespoons chicken soup base or bouillon granules
- ¼ teaspoon ground nutmeg

 Ready-Made Meal Assembly

In each of 8 Mylar bags, tote bags, or vacuum bags, store:

- 1 bag soup mix
- 1 bag creamy mix

 Label each bag

Combine the soup mix and 6 cups of water in a large pot over medium heat. Simmer for 30 minutes. Combine the creamy mix with 2 cups of water and stir into soup. Simmer 10 minutes, until thickened, and serve. Serves 8.

Cream of Cauliflower Soup

This is a very creamy, delicious cauliflower soup made more robust with the addition of potato flakes. The sour cream adds a really nice tanginess. This is awesome served with Cheddar Garlic Biscuits (page 126) or rolls, and if you have any leftover bread, you can make crispy croutons to float on top.

Makes 8 (6-serving) meals

Ingredients

2 cups chicken soup base or bouillon granules, divided

20 cups potato flakes

20 cups dehydrated cauliflower

4 cups dehydrated onion

2 cups dehydrated celery

1 tablespoon plus 1 teaspoon white pepper

2 teaspoons ground coriander

1 teaspoon ground nutmeg

2 cups dry milk

2 cups sour cream powder

Instructions

For soup mix: In each of 8 vacuum bags or jars, add and then seal:

- 1 tablespoon chicken soup base or bouillon granules
- 2½ cups potato flakes
- 2½ cups dehydrated cauliflower
- ½ cup dehydrated onion
- ¼ cup dehydrated celery
- ½ teaspoon white pepper
- ¼ teaspoon ground coriander
- ⅛ teaspoon ground nutmeg

For creamy mix: In each of 8 vacuum bags or zip-top bags, add and then seal:

- ¼ cup dry milk
- ¼ cup sour cream powder
- 1 tablespoon chicken soup base or bouillon granules

 Ready-Made Meal Assembly

In each of 8 Mylar bags, tote bags, or vacuum bags, store:

- 1 bag soup mix
- 1 bag creamy mix

To package in a jar: Put the soup mix in the bottom of the jar. Package the creamy mix in zip-top bags and place on top.

 Label each bag

In a large saucepan, heat 8 cups of water over medium-high heat until nearly boiling. Add the soup mix and stir, breaking up any lumps. Simmer gently for about 20 minutes, until vegetables are rehydrated and tender. Add the creamy mix and stir until dissolved and heated through. Taste. Add salt if needed and serve. Serves 6.

Broccoli Cheddar Soup

Everyone loves this classic soup. Break this out on a chilly day and you've got a sure-fire winner.

Makes 8 (8-serving) meals

Ingredients

24 cups dehydrated broccoli

8 cups dehydrated onion

8 cups dehydrated diced potato

2 cups chicken soup base or bouillon granules

2⅔ cups sour cream powder

2⅔ cups dry milk

2⅔ cups flour

4 pounds cheddar cheese

8 (½-pint) chunks of cheddar cheese canned, vacuum-packed, or waxed (page 22), or 8 cups freeze-dried cheddar cheese

Instructions

For soup mix: In each of 8 vacuum bags, add and then seal:

- 3 cups dehydrated broccoli
- 1 cup dehydrated onion
- 1 cup dehydrated diced potato
- ¼ cup chicken soup base or bouillon granules

For creamy mix: In each of 8 vacuum bags, add and then seal:

- ⅓ cup sour cream powder
- ⅓ cup dry milk
- ⅓ cup flour

Ready-Made Meal Assembly

In each of 8 Mylar bags, tote bags, or vacuum bags, store:

- 1 bag soup mix
- 1 bag creamy mix
- 1 packet cheese

Label each bag

In a large pot, combine the soup mix and 12 cups of water over medium-high heat. Simmer gently for 30 minutes, until broccoli is tender. Meanwhile grate or cube the cheese. Stir the creamy mix and cheese into the soup and simmer and stir for 10 minutes or until thickened. Puree soup or process through a food mill and serve. Serves 8.

Carrot Ginger Soup

This is a lovely sweet and tangy carrot soup. The potatoes give it an extra oomph and the sour cream powder adds a wonderful creaminess.

Makes 8 (8-serving) meals

Ingredients

24 cups dehydrated carrots

8 cups dehydrated onion

8 cups dehydrated diced potato

2 cups chicken soup base or bouillon granules

2 tablespoons plus 1 teaspoon ground ginger

4 cups sour cream powder

4 cups dry milk

Instructions

For soup mix: In each of 8 vacuum bags, add and then seal:

- 3 cups dehydrated carrots
- 1 cup dehydrated onion
- 1 cup dehydrated diced potato
- ¼ cup chicken soup base or bouillon granules
- 2 teaspoons ground ginger

For creamy mix: In each of 8 vacuum bags, add and then seal:

- ½ cup sour cream powder
- ½ cup dry milk

Ready-Made Meal Assembly
In each of 8 Mylar bags, tote bags, or vacuum bags, store:

- 1 bag soup mix
- 1 bag creamy mix

Label each bag
In a large pot over medium-high heat, combine the soup mix and 10 cups of water. Simmer gently for 30 minutes, until carrots are tender. Stir in the creamy mix and serve. Serves 8.

Nourishing Beef, Lentil, Brown Rice, and Noodle Soup

This soup just has so many satisfying tastes and textures, it really fills you up and stays with you.

Makes 8 (8-serving) bags

Ingredients

2⅔ cups beef soup base or bouillon granules

4 cups dehydrated chopped onion

4 cups dehydrated chopped carrots

4 cups dried split peas

4 cups dried barley

4 cups dried lentils

4 cups uncooked brown rice

8 pints Home-Canned Beef (page 48) or 8 cups freeze-dried beef, sausage, or TVP

16 cups egg noodles or other pasta

Instructions

For soup mix: In each of 8 vacuum bags or jars, add and then seal:

- ⅓ cup beef soup base or bouillon granules
- ½ cup dehydrated chopped onion
- ½ cup dehydrated chopped carrots
- ½ cup dried split peas
- ½ cup dried barley
- ½ cup dried lentils
- ½ cup uncooked brown rice
- 1 cup freeze-dried beef, sausage, or TVP (if using freeze-dried)

For noodles: In each of 8 zip-top bags add and then seal:

- 2 cups egg noodles or other pasta

Ready-Made Meal Assembly

In each of 8 Mylar bags, tote bags, or vacuum bags, store:

- 1 bag soup mix
- 1 bag noodles
- 1 pint jar or retort pouch home-canned beef chunks (if using home-canned)

Label each bag

Combine the soup mix and 12 cups of water in a large pot over medium-high heat and simmer for 45 minutes. Add the beef and noodles and cook for 10 minutes more, or until the noodles are tender. Serves 8.

Potato, Chive, and Cheddar Soup

All the flavors of a stuffed baked potato make for a tasty, filling soup. A ½-pint jar of home-canned bacon, crisped and crumbled, takes this soup over the top.

Makes 8 (6-serving) meals

Ingredients

2 cups chicken soup base or bouillon granules, divided

24 cups potato flakes

4 cups dehydrated chopped onion

2 cups dehydrated chopped celery

½ cup dried chives

½ cup onion powder

4 teaspoons pepper

2 cups dry milk

2 cups sour cream powder

2 pounds cheddar cheese, home-canned into 8 (¼-pint) jars or cut into 4-ounce chunks and waxed, or 8 cups freeze-dried cheddar cheese

2 pounds bacon, home-canned into ½-pint jars or 2 cups bacon bits (optional)

Instructions

For soup mix: In each of 8 vacuum bags or jars, add and then seal:

- 3 tablespoons chicken soup base or bouillon granules
- 3 cups potato flakes
- ½ cup dehydrated chopped onion
- ¼ cup dehydrated chopped celery
- 1 tablespoon dried chives
- 1 tablespoon onion powder
- ½ teaspoon pepper
- ¼ cup dry milk
- ¼ cup sour cream powder
- 1 cup freeze-dried cheddar cheese (if using freeze-dried)

For bacon (optional): If using bacon bits, package into 8 zip-top bags:

- ¼ cup bacon bits

 Ready-Made Meal Assembly

In each of 8 Mylar bags, tote bags, or vacuum bags, store:

- 1 vacuum bag soup mix
- 1 jar cheese (if using home-canned)
- 1 jar bacon or 1 bag bacon bits

To prepare in a jar: Put the soup mix in the bottom of the jar. Package the jar of cheese on top (if using).

 Label each bag
Combine the soup mix and 12 cups of water over medium-high heat and simmer for 45 minutes. Grate the cheese or reconstitute in cool water and drain. Add half the cheese to the soup and stir to melt. [If using canned bacon, add "In a skillet, cook the bacon until crisp, and then crumble."] Serve garnished with the remaining cheese and the bacon. Serves 6.

Turkey and Mushroom Noodle Soup Mix

The sage and thyme in this soup always make me think of Thanksgiving leftovers. It's homey and comforting.

Makes 8 (8-serving) meals

Ingredients

8 cups tiny egg noodles or spaghetti, broken into 1-inch lengths

6 cups dehydrated onion

6 cups dehydrated celery

6 cups dehydrated carrots

6 cups dehydrated mushrooms

1 cup chicken soup base or bouillon granules

1½ tablespoons pepper

1½ tablespoons dried thyme

1 tablespoon dried sage

2 teaspoons celery seeds

2 teaspoons garlic powder

8 bay leaves

8 slices dehydrated lemon

16 cups turkey or chicken, cubed and lightly browned (if using home-canned) or 8 cups freeze-dried turkey, chicken, or sausage

Instructions

For soup mix: In each of 8 vacuum bags or jars, add and then seal:

- 1 cup tiny egg noodles or spaghetti, broken into 1-inch lengths
- ¾ cup dehydrated onion
- ¾ cup dehydrated celery
- ¾ cup dehydrated carrots
- ¾ cup dehydrated mushrooms
- 2 tablespoons chicken soup base or bouillon granules
- ½ teaspoon pepper
- ½ teaspoon dried thyme
- ¼ teaspoon dried sage
- ⅛ teaspoon celery seeds
- ⅛ teaspoon garlic powder
- 1 bay leaf
- 1 slice dehydrated lemon

For turkey or chicken: If using home-canned, cube the turkey or chicken and lightly brown in a pan. Using a canning funnel, divide the turkey or chicken among 8 pint-size sterilized jars or retort pouches. Cover with water and leave 1 inch headspace for jars, 2 inches for pouches. Seal the pouches or jars and pressure-can for 75 minutes. If using freeze-dried, vacuum seal ½ cup in each of 8 bags.

Ready-Made Meal Assembly
In each of 8 Mylar bags, tote bags, or vacuum bags, store:

- 1 vacuum bag soup mix
- 1 jar or pouch turkey or chicken

Label each bag
Simmer the soup mix and the contents of the turkey or chicken pouch in a large pot over medium-high heat with 8 cups of water for 15 minutes or until noodles and vegetables are tender. Serves 8.

Chicken Noodle Soup

There's nothing quite as homey and satisfying as a bowl of chicken soup. This recipe uses a tiny touch of lemon to just brighten the flavors. A wonderful soup to have on hand, serve to a loved one with a cold, or give as a gift to someone who is recuperating. It is nourishing, loving, and healing.

Makes 8 (8-serving) meals

Ingredients

4 pounds chicken breasts, thighs, or a combination, lightly browned and chopped

3 cups chopped onion

3 cups peeled and chopped carrots

3 cups chopped celery

1 cup chicken soup stock

8 slices dehydrated lemon

5 tablespoons plus 1 teaspoon dried thyme

8 bay leaves

16 cups egg noodles

Instructions

For soup mix: In each of 8 quart-size canning jars or retort pouches, add, seal, and then pressure-can for 75 minutes:

- 1 cup chopped lightly browned chicken
- ¾ cup chopped onion
- ¾ cup peeled and chopped carrots
- ¾ cup chopped celery
- 2 tablespoons chicken soup stock
- 1 slice dehydrated lemon
- 2 teaspoons dried thyme
- 1 bay leaf
- Water, to cover and leave 1 inch of headspace in a 1-quart jar, or 2 inches in a retort pouch

For noodle packet: In each of 8 vacuum bags, add and then seal:

- 2 cups egg noodles

Ready-Made Meal Assembly

In each of 8 Mylar bags, tote bags, or vacuum bags, store:

- 1-quart jar or retort pouch chicken soup mix
- 1 packet noodles

Label each bag

Combine the chicken soup mix and 12 cups of water in a large pot over medium heat. Bring to a simmer and add the noodles. Simmer for about 10 minutes, or until the noodles are tender. Remove the bay leaf and lemon slice, and serve. Serves 8.

Chicken Rice Soup

Bright with the flavor of lemon and thyme, this soup is healing, homey, and delicious.

Makes 8 (8-serving) meals

Ingredients

4 pounds chicken breasts, thighs, or a combination, lightly browned and chopped

3 cups chopped onion

3 cups peeled and chopped carrots

3 cups chopped celery

1 cup chicken soup stock

8 slices dehydrated lemon

5 tablespoons plus 1 teaspoon dried thyme

8 bay leaves

12 cups uncooked white rice

Instructions

For soup mix: In each of 8 quart-size canning jars or retort pouches, add, seal, and then pressure-can for 75 minutes:

- 1 cup chopped lightly browned chicken, chopped
- ¾ cup chopped onion
- ¾ cup peeled and chopped carrots
- ¾ cup chopped celery
- 2 tablespoons of chicken soup stock
- 1 slice of dehydrated lemon
- 2 teaspoons dried thyme
- 1 bay leaf
- Water to leave 1 inch headspace in a 1-quart jar, or 2 inches in a retort pouch

For rice packet: In each of 8 vacuum bags, add and then seal:

- 1½ cups uncooked white rice

Ready-Made Meal Assembly

In each of 8 Mylar bags, tote bags, or vacuum bags, store:

- 1-quart jar or retort pouch chicken soup mix
- 1 packet rice

Label each bag

Combine the chicken soup mix and 12 cups of water in a large pot over medium heat. Bring to a simmer and add the rice. Simmer for about 20 minutes, until rice is done. Remove the bay leaf and lemon slice, and serve. Serves 8.

Chunky Beef Soup with Barley and Tomato

This combination of peas, barley, and lentils together with beef and tomatoes simmers for just about 40 minutes into a super hungry-man filler-upper.

Makes 8 (8-serving) meals

Ingredients

6 cups dried split peas

2 cups beef soup base or bouillon granules

6 cups uncooked pearl barley

6 cups dried lentils

4 cups dried minced onion

½ cup Italian seasoning

12 cups uncooked long-grain white rice

8 pounds beef chunks, lightly browned and home-canned (page 48) or 12 cups freeze-dried beef, sausage, or TVP

8 (28-ounce) cans diced tomatoes with juice

Instructions

For soup mix: In each of 8 quart-sized sterilized canning jars or retort pouches, add and then seal:

- ¾ cup dried split peas
- ¼ cup beef soup base or bouillon granules
- ¾ cup uncooked pearl barley
- ¾ cup dried lentils
- ½ cup dried minced onion
- 1 tablespoon Italian seasoning
- 1½ cups uncooked long-grain white rice
- 1½ cups freeze-dried beef, sausage or, TVP (if using; if it does not fit in the jar or pouch, package it separately)

Ready-Made Meal Assembly

In each of 8 Mylar bags, tote bags, or vacuum bags, store:

- 1-quart jar or pouch soup mix
- 1 can tomatoes
- 1-pint jar or pouch beef (if using)

Label each bag

Combine the soup mix and tomatoes in a large with 12 cups of water. Simmer about 40 minutes. Add the beef and cook 10 minutes more. Serves 8.

Chicken Chipotle Soup

This slightly spicy chicken and chili soup is a delightful change of pace, and the crunchy corn chip topping is a favorite.

Makes 8 (8-serving) meals

Ingredients

8 cups black beans, soaked overnight

6 cups chopped onion

½ cup dried or granulated garlic

4 pounds boneless, skinless chicken thighs, chopped and lightly browned

2 tablespoons plus 2 teaspoons paprika

2 tablespoons plus 2 teaspoons dried oregano

2 cups chicken soup base or bouillon granules

8 cups frozen corn kernels

1½ cups chopped canned chipotle chiles in adobo

½ cup adobo sauce (optional)

½ cup salt

5 tablespoons plus 1 teaspoon dried cilantro

8 slices dehydrated lemon

8 (28-ounce) cans diced tomatoes with juice

16 cups lightly crushed corn chips

Instructions

For soup mix: In each of 8 quart-size canning jars or retort pouches, add, seal, and then pressure-can 75 minutes:

- 1 cup black beans, soaked overnight
- ¾ cup chopped onion
- 1 tablespoon dried or granulated garlic
- 1 cups boneless, skinless chicken thighs, chopped and lightly browned
- 1 teaspoon paprika
- 1 teaspoon dried oregano
- ¼ cup chicken soup base or bouillon granules
- 1 cup frozen corn kernels
- 3 tablespoons chopped canned chipotle chiles in adobo
- 1 tablespoon adobo sauce (optional)
- 1 tablespoon salt
- 2 teaspoons dried cilantro
- 1 slice dehydrated lemon
- Water, to cover and leave 1 inch of headspace in a 1-quart jar, or 2 inches in a retort pouch

For corn chips: In each of 8 vacuum bags, add and then seal:

- 2 cups lightly crushed corn chips

 Ready-Made Meal Assembly
In each of 8 Mylar bags, tote bags, or vacuum bags, store:

- 1-quart jar or retort pouch soup mix
- 1 can tomatoes
- 1 bag corn chips

 Label each bag
Combine the soup mix and tomatoes in a large pot with 6 cups of water over medium-high heat. Simmer until heated through and flavors meld, about 30 minutes. Remove the lemon slice. Serve topped with corn chips. Serves 8.

Creamy Wild Rice Soup

Wild rice adds a toothsome, nutty quality to this creamy soup.

Makes 8 (8-serving) meals

Ingredients

8 cups finely chopped onion

8 cups finely chopped peeled carrots

8 cups finely chopped celery

½ cup olive oil

1 tablespoon plus 1 teaspoon salt

2 teaspoons pepper

1 cup chicken soup base or bouillon granules

6 cups wild rice

8 slices dehydrated lemon

1 cup dried parsley

2 cups flour

2⅔ cups dry milk

8 cups sliced almonds (optional)

Instructions

In multiple batches if necessary, sauté the onions, carrots, and celery in oil for about 20 minutes, until starting to turn golden.

For soup base: In each of 8 quart-size canning jars or retort pouches, add, seal, and then pressure-can for 25 minutes:

- 3 cups sautéed vegetables
- 1 teaspoon salt
- ½ teaspoon pepper
- 2 tablespoons chicken soup base or bouillon granules
- Water, to cover and leave 1 inch of headspace in a 1-quart jar, or 2 inches in a retort pouch

For wild rice: In each of 8 vacuum or zip-top bags, add and then seal:

- ¾ cup wild rice
- 1 slice dehydrated lemon
- 2 tablespoons dried parsley

For creamy mix: In each of 8 vacuum or zip-top bags, add and then seal:

- ¼ cup flour
- ⅔ cup dry milk

For almonds (if using): In each of 8 vacuum or zip-top bags, add and then seal:

- 1 cup sliced almonds

 Ready-Made Meal Assembly
In each of 8 Mylar bags, tote bags, or vacuum bags, store:

- 1 bag soup base
- 1 bag wild rice
- 1 bag creamy mix
- 1 bag almonds

 Label each bag
Combine the soup base, 6 cups of water, and the rice packet contents in a large pot over medium heat. Bring to a simmer and cook for 40 minutes. Remove the lemon slice. In a small bowl, stir together the creamy mix and 1 cup of water. Add to the soup and simmer for 10 more minutes, stirring frequently. Toast the almonds in a small pan until fragrant and slightly golden, about 5 minutes. Serve the soup sprinkled with almonds. Serves 8.

Lentil Soup

Lentils are one of the quickest cooking of the nutritious legume (bean) family. This classic soup is very filling.

Makes 8 (8-serving) meals

Ingredients

12 cups lentils

6 cups dehydrated carrots

6 cups dehydrated onion

6 cups dehydrated celery

1 cup chicken soup base or bouillon granules

½ cup salt

¼ cup pepper

5 tablespoons plus 1 teaspoon dried garlic

4 teaspoons dried thyme

8 bay leaves

8 (15-ounce) cans diced tomatoes

Instructions

For soup mix: In each of 8 vacuum bags, add and then seal:

- 1½ cups lentils
- ¾ cup dehydrated carrots
- ¾ cup dehydrated onion
- ¾ cup dehydrated celery
- 2 tablespoons chicken soup base or bouillon granules
- 1 tablespoon salt
- ½ tablespoon pepper
- 2 teaspoons dried garlic
- ½ teaspoon dried thyme
- 1 bay leaf

 Ready-Made Meal Assembly
In each of 8 Mylar bags, tote bags, or vacuum bags, store:

- 1 bag soup mix
- 1 can diced tomatoes

 Label each bag
In a slow cooker or soup pot, combine all the ingredients and 8 cups of water. Simmer on medium-high heat for 1 hour, or until the lentils are tender. Serves 8.

Armenian Lentil Soup

Armenian Lentil Soup includes cinnamon and dried fruit that add a bit of sweetness and a nice flavor contrast to this savory soup. It cooks in about 45 minutes, so it is a perfect choice when you don't want to do a long simmer.

Makes 8 (8-serving) meals

Ingredients

4 cups dehydrated onion

4 tablespoons ground ginger

2 tablespoons plus 2 teaspoons ground cinnamon

½ cup salt

10⅔ cups red lentils

1 cup chicken soup base or bouillon granules

6 cups dried apricots, diced

6 cups golden raisins

3 cups sour cream powder

8 (14.5-ounce) cans diced tomatoes

Instructions

For soup mix: In each of 8 vacuum bags or jars, add and then seal:

- ½ cup dehydrated onion
- 1½ teaspoons ground ginger
- 1 teaspoon ground cinnamon
- 1 tablespoon salt
- 1⅓ cups red lentils
- 2 tablespoons chicken soup base or bouillon granules

For dried fruit: In each of 8 zip-top bags, add:

- ¾ cup dried apricots, diced
- ¾ cup golden raisins

For sour cream: In each of 8 zip-top plastic bags, add and then seal:

- ½ cup sour cream powder

 ### Ready-Made Meal Assembly
In each of 8 Mylar bags, tote bags, or vacuum bags, store:

- 1 bag soup mix
- 1 can diced tomatoes
- 1 bag dried fruit
- 1 packet sour cream powder

 Label each bag
In a large pot over medium-low heat, combine the soup packet, tomatoes, and 8 cups of water. Simmer for 30 minutes, or until the lentils are almost tender. Stir in the dried fruit and cook 10 more minutes. Mix the sour cream powder with ¼ cup of water. Serve the soup topped with a drizzle of sour cream. Serves 8.

Mexican Bean Soup

Yummy, spicy, and chili-like, this soup is a huge favorite of the guys. It's served garnished with shredded cheese and would also be delicious with a smattering of Fritos corn chips on top. Be sure to start soaking the beans the night before serving.

Makes 8 (8-serving) meals

Ingredients

6 cups dried kidney beans

6 cups dried pinto beans

1 cup dehydrated onion

3 tablespoons red pepper flakes

2 tablespoons plus 2 teaspoons dried garlic or garlic granules

3 tablespoons chicken soup base or bouillon granules

½ cup tomato powder

½ teaspoon black pepper

2 pounds cheddar cheese, vacuum-packed, waxed, or canned in 8 (4-ounce) servings (page 22)

Instructions

For beans: In each of 8 vacuum bags or jars, add and then seal:

- ¾ cup dried kidney beans
- ¾ cup dried pinto beans

For seasoning packet: In each of 8 vacuum or zip-top bags, add and then seal:

- 2 tablespoons dehydrated onion
- 1 teaspoon red pepper flakes
- 1 teaspoon dried garlic or garlic granules
- 3 tablespoons chicken soup base or bouillon granules
- 1 tablespoon tomato powder
- ½ teaspoon black pepper

Ready-Made Meal Assembly
In each of 8 Mylar bags, tote bags, or vacuum bags, store:

- 1 bag beans
- 1 seasoning packet
- 1 bag, can, or waxed chunk cheese

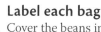
Label each bag
Cover the beans in water and soak overnight, then drain and rinse. Combine the beans and seasoning packet in a large soup pot with 9 cups of water. Bring to a boil over high heat and boil for 10 minutes. Reduce the heat to a simmer and cook 45 to 60 minutes, until the beans are tender. Let cool, and then puree or process in a food processor or food mill. Return to the pot, reheat, and serve topped with grated cheese. Serves 8.

Pasta e Fagioli

This is a delicious Italian soup with a bit of spice from the red pepper flakes.

Makes 8 (8-serving) bags

Ingredients

2 cups chicken soup base or bouillon granules

12 cups dehydrated onion

8 cups dehydrated celery

8 cup dehydrated carrots

½ cup dried rosemary

¼ cup dried garlic or garlic powder

4 teaspoons red pepper flakes

8 bay leaves

16 cups dried cannellini beans

16 cups rigatone, penne, or other short tube pasta

8 (28-ounce) cans diced tomatoes

Instructions

For soup mix: In each of 8 vacuum bags, add and then seal:

- ¼ cup chicken soup base or bouillon granules
- 1½ cups dehydrated onion
- 1 cups dehydrated celery
- 1 cup dehydrated carrots
- 1 tablespoon dried rosemary
- 2 teaspoons dried garlic or garlic powder
- ½ teaspoon red pepper flakes
- 1 bay leaf

For beans: In each of 8 zip-top bags, add and then seal:

- 2 cups dried cannellini beans

For pasta: In each of 8 vacuum or zip-top bags, add and then seal:

2 cups short tube pasta

Ready-Made Meal Assembly

In each of 8 Mylar bags, tote bags, or vacuum bags, store:

- 1 bag soup mix
- 1 bag beans
- 1 bag pasta
- 1 can diced tomatoes

Label each bag

Cover the beans with water and soak overnight, then drain and rinse. In a large pot, combine the beans, soup mix, and 12 cups of water over medium-high heat. Simmer for 60 minutes, or until the beans are almost tender. Add the tomatoes and pasta and cook 10 minutes more. Remove the bay leaf and serve. Serves 8.

Split Pea Soup

This is a super-easy classic soup. Start it early and let it slowly simmer for much of the day. It only gets better when the flavor of the ham permeates the peas.

Makes (8-serving) meals

Ingredients

16 cups dried green split peas

6 cups dehydrated carrots

6 cups dehydrated onion

6 cups dehydrated celery

1 cup chicken soup base or bouillon granules

½ cup salt

¼ cup pepper

5 tablespoons plus 1 teaspoon dried garlic

4 teaspoons Italian seasoning

8 bay leaves

8 (1-pint) jars or retort pouches home-canned diced ham, or 8 cups of freeze-dried diced ham

Instructions

For soup mix: In each of 8 vacuum bags, add and then seal:

- 2 cups dried green split peas
- ¾ cup dehydrated carrots
- ¾ cup dehydrated onion
- ¾ cup dehydrated celery
- 2 tablespoons chicken soup base or bouillon granules
- 1 tablespoon salt
- ½ tablespoon pepper
- 2 teaspoons dried garlic
- ½ teaspoon Italian seasoning
- 1 bay leaf
- 1 cup freeze-dried ham (if using freeze-dried)

 Ready-Made Meal Assembly
In each of 8 Mylar bags, tote bags, or vacuum bags, store:

- 1 bag of soup mix
- 1 pint or retort pouch home-canned ham (if using home-canned)

 Label each bag
In a slow cooker or soup pot, combine all the ingredients and 8 cups of water. Simmer on the lowest heat for up to 8 hours, or until peas are completely tender. Serves 8.

Tomato Soup with Cheese and Croutons

Tomato soup is a favorite in our house, and my family gets crazy with the toppings. Sometimes we add shredded cheddar and tiny fish-shaped crackers, but our favorite topping is garlicky croutons and a big sprinkle of Parmesan cheese. The croutons soften in the soup and the cheese melts, forming a cheesy raft that floats on the soup.

Makes 8 (8-serving) meals

Ingredients

8 cups dehydrated onions

2 cups beef soup base or bouillon granules

2 tablespoons plus 2 teaspoons dried thyme

16 bay leaves

2⅔ cups dry milk

2⅔ cups sour cream powder

6 cups finely grated Parmesan cheese (like Kraft brand)

6 cups croutons

16 (28-ounce) cans crushed tomatoes

Instructions

For soup mix: In each of 8 vacuum bags, add and then seal:

- 1 cup dehydrated onions
- ¼ cup beef soup base or bouillon granules
- 1 teaspoon dried thyme
- 2 bay leaves

For creamy mix: In each of 8 vacuum bags, add and then seal:

- ⅓ cup dry milk
- ⅓ cup sour cream powder

For cheese: In each of 8 vacuum bags, add and then seal:

- ¾ cup finely grated Parmesan cheese

For croutons: In each of 8 vacuum bags, add and then seal:

- ¾ cup croutons

Ready-Made Meal Assembly

In each of 8 Mylar bags, tote bags, or vacuum bags, store:

- 2 (28-ounce) cans crushed tomatoes
- 1 bag soup mix
- 1 bag creamy mix
- 1 bag croutons
- 1 bag Parmesan cheese

Label each bag

In a large soup pot, combine the tomatoes, soup mix, and 6 cups of water. Simmer 1 hour over medium-high heat. Puree the soup with a hand blender or through a food mill. In a small bowl, combine creamy mix and ⅓ cup of water. Stir the creamy mix into the soup and reheat if needed. Serve hot soup topped with croutons and cheese. Serves 8.

Tortilla Soup

This is a tangy soup that packs a big flavor punch. Do a test batch first and see how much spice you like and then scale up accordingly. I love to have this soup on hand and just whip it up after a hectic day at work because it's super-fast and easy, and everybody likes it.

Makes 8 (8-serving) meals

Ingredients

16 cups uncooked white rice

2⅔ cups chicken soup base or bouillon granules

½ cup red pepper flakes

16 dehydrated lemon slices

4 pounds Jack or cheddar cheese, canned in ½-pints, vacuum-sealed or waxed in 8-ounce chunks, or 8 cups freeze-dried Jack or cheddar cheese

16 cups lightly crushed tortilla chips

8 (28-ounce) cans diced tomatoes, preferably with chiles

Instructions

For soup mix: In each of 8 vacuum bags, add and then seal:

- 2 cups uncooked white rice
- ⅓ cup chicken soup base or bouillon granules
- 1 tablespoon red pepper flakes
- 2 dehydrated lemon slices
- 1 cup freeze-dried cheese (if using freeze-dried)

For tortilla chips: In each of 8 vacuum bags, add and then seal:

- 2 cups lightly crushed tortilla chips

Ready-Made Meal Assembly

In each of 8 Mylar bags, tote bags, or vacuum bags, store:

- 1 bag soup mix
- 1 bag tortilla chips
- 1 (28-ounce) can diced tomatoes
- 1 ½-pint canned cheese or 8-ounce waxed or vacuum-sealed Jack or cheddar cheese (if using)

Label each bag

In a large pot, combine the tomatoes, soup mix, and 12 cups of water. Simmer for 20 minutes over medium-high heat. Meanwhile, grate the cheese. Stir in half the tortilla chips. Serve the soup topped with the remaining chips and grated cheese. Serves 8.

Beefy Brown Rice and Vegetable

The brown rice adds a nutty and filling flavor to this lovely beef soup. I like to serve it with a side of Cheddar Garlic Biscuits (page 126).

Makes 8 (8-serving) meals

Ingredients

12 cups dehydrated broccoli

6 cups dehydrated carrots

6 cups dehydrated onion

6 cups dehydrated celery

8 cups uncooked brown rice

1 cup beef soup base or bouillon granules

½ cup salt

¼ cup pepper

5 tablespoons plus 1 teaspoon dried garlic

4 teaspoons dried thyme

8 bay leaves

8 (15-ounce) cans diced tomatoes

Instructions

For soup mix: In each of 8 vacuum bags, add and then seal:

- 1½ cups dehydrated broccoli
- ¾ cup dehydrated carrots
- ¾ cup dehydrated onion
- ¾ cup dehydrated celery
- 1 cup uncooked brown rice
- 2 tablespoons beef soup base or bouillon granules
- 1 tablespoon salt
- ½ tablespoon pepper
- 2 teaspoons dried garlic
- ½ teaspoon dried thyme
- 1 bay leaf

Ready-Made Meal Assembly
In each of 8 Mylar bags, tote bags, or vacuum bags, store:

- 1 bag soup mix
- 1 can tomatoes

Label each bag
In a large pot, combine all the ingredients and 8 cups of water. Simmer over medium-high heat for 50 minutes or until rice is cooked through.

Chapter 6
Primarily Pasta

Macaroni and Cheese 4 Ways

Mac and cheese is the epitome of comfort food, the favorite of all children and secret indulgence of many adults. This version is really delicious and creamy with a crunchy breadcrumb topping, the kind that nestles into a pile on your plate when it's hot and can be cut into squares after it has cooled. This particular recipe will make four versions: plain macaroni and cheese, macaroni and cheese with broccoli, macaroni and cheese with ham, and macaroni and cheese with ground beef. I might consider making a double batch and storing up 4 of each kind. These ready-made meals are universal family favorites.

Makes 8 (8-serving) bags

Ingredients

⅔ cup salt, divided

2⅔ cups butter-flavored vegetable shortening

2 tablespoons plus 2 teaspoons dry mustard

2 tablespoons plus 2 teaspoons garlic granules

2½ teaspoons cayenne pepper

2½ teaspoons black pepper

3 cups flour

½ cup chicken bouillon granules

10 cups dry milk

8 pounds Colby cheese, shredded

4 pounds extra-sharp cheddar cheese

4 cups dehydrated broccoli

6 cups dry breadcrumbs

8 pounds macaroni or other short tube-shaped pasta

2 (1-pint) jars home-canned diced ham (pressure-canned for 75 minutes) or 4 cups freeze-dried ham

2 (1-pint) jars Home-Canned Beef (page 48) (pressure-canned for 75 minutes) or 4 cups freeze-dried beef, sausage, or TVP

Instructions

For sauce step 1: In each of 8 vacuum bags, add and then seal:

- 1 teaspoon salt
- ⅓ cup shortening
- 1 teaspoon dry mustard
- 1 teaspoon garlic granules
- ¼ teaspoon cayenne pepper
- ¼ teaspoon black pepper
- 6 tablespoons flour

For sauce step 2: In each of 8 vacuum bags, add and then seal:

- 1 tablespoon chicken bouillon granules
- 1¼ cups dry milk

For cheese: If canning the cheese, shred the Colby and the cheddar separately. Seal the Colby in 8 pint-size jars and the cheddar in 8 ½-pint jars. Or, wax or vacuum-seal the Colby cheese in 1-pound chunks, and the cheddar in ½-pound chunks.

For broccoli: In each of 2 vacuum bags, add and then seal:

- 2 cups dehydrated broccoli

For breadcrumb topping: In each of 8 vacuum bags, add and then seal:

- ¾ cup breadcrumbs

 Ready-Made Meal Assembly
In each of 8 Mylar bags, tote bags or vacuum bags store:

- 1 pound macaroni or other
- Sauce Step 1 packet
- Sauce Step 2 packet
- 1 pint or pound Colby cheese
- ½-pint or pound cheddar cheese
- 2 cups broccoli for 2 of them
- 1 packet breadcrumbs
- 1 pint home-canned beef (or 2 cups freeze-dried beef) for 2 of them
- 1 pint ham (or 2 cups ham) for 2 of them

Label each bag

Preheat the oven to 375°F. Bring a large pot of water to a boil and cook macaroni (and broccoli, if included) and salt until just al dente, about 7 minutes; drain. Meanwhile, in a second large pot over medium-high heat, add sauce packet 1 and stir to melt the shortening. Cook about 2 minutes, stirring, and then add $5\frac{1}{5}$ cups of water and sauce packet 2. Cook, stirring very often, until thickened. Meanwhile, grate or cube the cheese (and open and drain the ham or beef, if included). When the sauce mixture is thickened, turn off heat and stir in the cheese until melted. Add the macaroni (and the broccoli, ham, or beef, if included) and stir to combine. Pour into a 9 x 9-inch or 7 x 11-inch baking dish. Sprinkle the breadcrumbs on top. Bake for 25 minutes or until bubbly and brown at the edges. Serves 8.

Home-Canned Spaghetti Sauce

This quintessential spaghetti sauce recipe is super-versatile. It can be paired with any type or shape of pasta, mixed with ground beef or sausage, or used to top pizzas. Package it in the sizes your family uses. I like pints for spaghetti dinners and ½-pints for pizza nights. This recipe makes about nine pints total. I like to make five pints and eight ½-pints. Adding chipotle chiles in adobo can turn this into a deliciously spicy sauce. The spicy sauce is great paired with braised meats of served over pasta or polenta. It is also fantastic with shrimp and spooned over cheesy grits, one of my very favorite meals. You'll find #10 cans of tomatoes at any club store or restaurant supply, like Sam's Club, Costco, Smart and Final, or Cash and Carry.

Makes 9 pints

Ingredients

30 pounds tomatoes or 2 (#10) cans tomatoes (club store or restaurant supply)

¼ cup vegetable oil

1 cup chopped onions

5 cloves garlic, minced

1 cup chopped celery or green pepper

1 pound fresh mushrooms, sliced

4 tablespoons minced parsley

2 tablespoons dried oregano

4½ teaspoons salt

2 teaspoons black pepper

¼ cup brown sugar

1 to 2 (7-ounce) cans chipotle chiles in adobo sauce, pureed (optional)

Instructions

For fresh tomatoes, bring a large pot of water to a boil and dip the tomatoes in the boiling water until their skins split. Peel and set aside. Heat the oil in a large saucepan over medium-high heat and cook the onion, peppers or celery, and mushrooms until softened. Combine the cooked vegetables and all the remaining ingredients in a large pot over medium-high heat and simmer for at least 1 hour, until reduced and thick. Add to sterile pint jars, cap with lids and rings, and pressure-can for 20 minutes. Makes about 9 pints. Note: ½-pints are a great size to package in pizza kits.

Pasta and Sauce Ready-Made Meals

Pair spaghetti with garlic bread and you've got comfort on a plate. You can use your own home-canned spaghetti sauce or choose to purchase pint-sized cans of spaghetti sauce.

Makes 24 (4-serving) bags, 4 each in 6 varieties

Ingredients

24 (1-pint) jars Home-Canned Spaghetti Sauce (page 74) or store-bought spaghetti sauce

6 pounds Parmesan cheese

3 cups salt, packaged into 24 (2-tablespoon) packets

4 (1-pint) jars Home-Canned Beef (page 48) or 8 cups freeze-dried beef or TVP

4 (1-pint) jars home-canned crumbled Italian sausage or 8 cups freeze-dried sausage

24 (1-pound) bags pasta

4 (1-pint) jars home-canned meatballs

4 (6.5-ounce) cans store-bought canned clams

4 (6-ounce) cans store-bought black olives

Instructions

For spaghetti sauce: Most commercial sauce is sold in quart-size jars or cans. This is enough to sauce 2 pounds of pasta and serve 8, so if you use store-bought sauce, you might choose to make meal kits to serve 8 instead of 4. Muir Glen and Eden Organic both package commercially canned spaghetti sauce in 16-ounce cans, which are a perfect size.

For cheese: You'll need 24 (4-ounce) servings of Parmesan to create all 24 ready-made meals. The cheese can be finely grated Parmesan vacuum-sealed into 4-ounce servings, or you can vacuum-seal or wax 4-ounce chunks of cheese and grate the cheese at time of use.

For salt: Divide the salt into 24 (2-tablespoon) portions and package each in a small zip-top bag.

For beef: If using freeze-dried beef or TVP, in each of 4 vacuum bags, add and then seal:

• 2 cups freeze-dried beef or TVP

For sausage: If using freeze-dried, in each of 4 vacuum bags, add and then seal:

• 2 cups freeze-dried sausage crumbles

Ready-Made Meal Assembly

In each of 8 Mylar bags, tote bags, or vacuum bags, store:

• 1 pound pasta
• 1 packet salt
• 1 pint spaghetti sauce

• 4 ounces Parmesan cheese
• 1 jar or bag each of beef, meatballs, sausage, clams, and olives (or omit for plain)

Label each bag

Fill a large pot two-thirds full with water and add salt. Bring to a boil over high heat and add the pasta. Cook until almost al dente, 6 to 10 minutes. Meanwhile, in a medium saucepan, warm the pasta sauce with any included meat or olives over medium-low heat. When the pasta is almost done, drain off most of the water (reserve about 1 cup in case you need to thin the sauce). Add the sauce to the drained pasta and stir to coat and finish cooking together. Serve the pasta topped with grated Parmesan cheese. Serves 4.

Macaroni and Beef in a Creamy Tomato Sauce aka Beefaroni

Yum, tender beef and pasta in a creamy tomato sauce. Every kid's favorite and loved by adults as well.

Makes 6 (6 to 8-serving) meals

Ingredients

6 pounds macaroni or other pasta shape

¾ cup salt

6 (1-pint) jars Home-Canned Spaghetti Sauce (page 74) or 6 (16-ounce) cans store-bought spaghetti sauce

6 (1-pint) jars Home-Canned Beef (page 48) or 12 cups freeze-dried beef, sausage, or TVP

3 cups sour cream powder

Instructions

For pasta: In each of 6 vacuum bags, add and then seal:

- 1 pound pasta
- 2 tablespoons salt

For freeze-dried meat (if using): In each of 6 vacuum bags, add and then seal:

- 2 cups freeze-dried beef, sausage, or TVP

For sour cream: In each of 6 vacuum bags, add and then seal:

- ½ cup sour cream powder

Ready-Made Meal Assembly
In each of 6 Mylar bags, tote bags, or vacuum bags, store:

- 1 pound of macaroni or other pasta shape and salt
- 1 jar spaghetti sauce
- 1 pint home-canned beef or 1 bag freeze-dried meat
- 1 bag cream powder

Label each bag
Bring a large pot of water to a boil and add salt. Cook the pasta until al dente, about 8 minutes. Meanwhile, in a separate pot over medium heat, warm the sauce and meat. When pasta is done, drain, reserving 1 cup of cooking water. In a small bowl, mix the sour cream powder with ¼ cup of water. Combine the pasta, sauce, and sour cream, toss to combine, and serve. Serves 6 to 8.

Baked Pasta Ready-Made Meals

The most basic yet satisfying of all casseroles is baked pasta. There are two ways to make this: You can boil the pasta on the stovetop and serve it casserole-style from the skillet, either baked in the oven or not; or, you can assemble a baking dish of all the ingredients, adding the pasta raw, and adding 2 cups of water. The pasta will absorb the extra water and become tender while it cooks. I love this approach, because rather than cleaning a pot, a colander, and a pan, I only have one baking dish to clean, and the whole thing cooks unattended. Yay for one-dish cooking!

Makes 16 (6 to 8-serving) meals, 4 each of 4 varieties

Ingredients

4 (1-pint) jars Home-Canned Beef (page 48) (ground or chunks) or 8 cups of freeze-dried beef or TVP

4 (1-pint) jars home-canned crumbled sausage or 8 cups freeze-dried sausage crumbles

6 cups dried mushrooms

2 pounds Parmesan cheese

16 (1-pound) bags pasta (a variety of shapes would be lovely)

16 (1-pint) jars Home-Canned Spaghetti Sauce (page 74) or store-bought spaghetti sauce

2 (24-ounce) bags individually packaged string cheese

4 (1-pint) jars home-canned meatballs

Instructions

For beef: If using freeze-dried beef or TVP, in each of 4 vacuum bags, add and then seal:

- 2 cups freeze-dried beef or TVP

For sausage: If using freeze-dried, in each of 4 vacuum bags, add and then seal:

- 2 cups freeze-dried sausage crumbles

For mushrooms: In each of 4 vacuum bags, add and then seal:

- 1½ cups dried mushrooms

For cheese: You'll need 16 (4-ounce) servings of Parmesan to create all 24 ready-made meals. The cheese can be finely grated Parmesan (like Kraft brand) vacuum-sealed into 4-ounce servings, or you can vacuum-seal or wax 4-ounce chunks of cheese and grate the cheese at time of use.

 Ready-Made Meal Assembly

In each of 16 Mylar bags, tote bags, or vacuum bags, store:

- 1 pound pasta
- 1 pint spaghetti sauce
- 3 packets string cheese
- 1 (4-ounce) package Parmesan cheese
- 1 pint or bag beef, sausage, or meatballs, or 1 bag mushrooms

 Label each bag
Preheat the oven to 400°F. Open and chop the string cheese. In a 9 x 13-inch baking dish, mix together all the ingredients (except the Parmesan cheese) and 2 cups of water. Bake for 1 hour. Stir. Top with grated Parmesan and bake 15 more minutes. Alternately, cook in a solar oven or wonder oven. Serves 6 to 8.

Creamy Baked Pasta Ready-Made Meals

Yum, creamy pasta and lovely sauce. This recipe works with either commercially jarred Alfredo sauce or with the packet of cream sauce mix included in this recipe. The cream sauce mix uses a combination of dry milk and powdered sour cream, which doesn't sound like much, but is actually quite delicious. I love that you can make 16 of these easily at once. That's both money-saving and time-saving.

Makes 16 (8-serving) meals, 4 each of 4 varieties

Ingredients

16 pints Alfredo sauce or $5\frac{1}{3}$ cups dry milk and $5\frac{1}{3}$ cups powdered sour cream

12 (1-pint) jars home-canned chicken or 24 cups freeze-dried chicken

4 (1-pint) home-canned diced ham or 8 cups freeze-dried ham

4 cups dehydrated mushrooms

18 cups dried peas

4 cups dehydrated broccoli

12 cups dry breadcrumbs

6 (1-pound) bags pasta (a variety of shapes would be lovely)

2 cups salt, packaged in 24 (2-tablespoon) portions in zip-top bags

4 cups finely grated Parmesan cheese (like Kraft brand)

Instructions

For sauce: If not using store-bought Alfredo sauce, in each of 16 vacuum bags, add and then seal:

- $\frac{2}{3}$ cup dry milk
- $\frac{2}{3}$ cup powdered sour cream

For chicken: If using freeze-dried, in each of 16 vacuum bags, add and then seal:

- 2 cups freeze-dried chicken

For ham: If using freeze-dried, in each of 4 vacuum bags, add and then seal:

- 2 cups freeze-dried ham

For mushrooms: In each of 4 vacuum bags, add and then seal:

- 1 cup dehydrated mushrooms

For peas: In each of 8 vacuum bags, add and then seal:

- 1 cup dried peas

For broccoli: In each of 4 vacuum bags, add and then seal:

- 1 cup dehydrated broccoli

For breadcrumb topping: In each of 16 vacuum bags, add and then seal:

- ¾ cup breadcrumbs
- ¼ cup finely grated Parmesan cheese

Ready-Made Meal Assembly

In each of 16 Mylar bags, tote bags, or vacuum bags, store:

- 1 pound pasta
- 1 bag salt

- 1 pint Alfredo sauce or 1 packet creamy mix
- 1 packet breadcrumb mix

To 4 bags add:

- 1 bag peas

To 4 bags add:

- 1 pint or bag chicken
- 1 bag broccoli

To 4 bags add:

- 1 pint or bag ham
- 1 bag peas

To 4 bags add:

- 1 pint or bag chicken
- 1 bag mushrooms

Label each bag

Fill a large pot three-quarters full with water, add salt, and bring to a boil over high heat. Place vegetables in a small pot and ladle a cup or two of boiling water over the vegetables, set on the stove, and let simmer over low heat for about 15 minutes or until they're rehydrated and tender. Meanwhile, add the pasta to the boiling water and cook until al dente. Open the package of ham or chicken and drain, reserving the juices. In a small pot, heat Alfredo sauce (if using prepared), or mix together powdered mix, reserved chicken or ham juices, and enough water (about 1 cup) to make a creamy sauce. Add the chicken or ham and the vegetables to the sauce and cook until heated through. Drain the pasta, reserving 1 cup pasta water. Combine the pasta and sauce, and stir to coat. Add the reserved water, as needed, to thin the sauce. Serve sprinkled with breadcrumb topping. Serves 8.

Pasta with Vegetable Sauce in 4 Varieties

"It's just vegetables and sauce," you say. "How good could that be?" Let me tell you: really good. The vegetables cook in salted water, then the pasta is cooked in the same water for added flavor. Then you mash the tender vegetables with lovely, buttery ghee (try it with brown butter ghee) and nutty Parmesan cheese and toss it with the pasta. Throw in a handful of buttery pistachios for crunch. Delicious!

Makes 16 (6 to 8-serving) meals, 4 each of 4 varieties

Ingredients

2 cups salt

8 cups dehydrated broccoli

8 cups dehydrated peas

8 cups dehydrated cauliflower

8 cups dehydrated mushrooms

2 pounds Parmesan cheese

8 cups shelled pistachios (optional) 16 (1-pound) bags pasta (a variety of shapes would be lovely)

16 (¼-pint) jars ghee (4 pounds total)

Instructions

For salt: In each of 16 small zip-top bags, add and then seal:

• 2 tablespoons salt

For vegetables: In each of 16 vacuum bags, add and then seal:

• 2 cups of one type of vegetable: broccoli, peas, cauliflower, or mushrooms

For cheese: You'll need 16 (4-ounce) servings of Parmesan to create all 24 ready-made meals. The cheese can be finely grated Parmesan (like Kraft brand) vacuum-sealed into 4-ounce servings, or you can vacuum-seal or wax 4-ounce chunks of cheese and grate the cheese at time of use.

For pistachios: In each of 16 vacuum bags, add and then seal:

• ½ cup (4 ounces) pistachios

 Ready-Made Meal Assembly

In each of 8 Mylar bags, tote bags, or vacuum bags, store:

• 1 pound pasta
• 1 bag salt
• 1 bag vegetables

• 1 jar ghee
• 1 package Parmesan cheese
• 1 bag pistachios (optional)

For all but mushroom bags:

Label each bag
Fill a large pot two-thirds full with water and add the salt. Warm over medium-high heat, and when hot, add the vegetables and bring to a low simmer. Cook until vegetables are very tender, 15 to 20 minutes. Using a big slotted spoon, fish out the vegetables and place in a large bowl near the stove to keep warm. Set the heat under the pot of water to high and bring to a boil, adding more water if needed to cook the pasta. Cook pasta until al dente. Meanwhile, drizzle the vegetables with the ghee and smash with the back of the spoon. Grate the cheese and add to the vegetables. When the pasta is done, reserve 1 cup of the cooking water. Drain the pasta and combine with the vegetable mixture. Toss to coat and add back as much of the reserved pasta water as needed to make a lovely sauce. Chop the pistachios, if using, and sprinkle on top of the pasta to serve. Serves 6 to 8.

For mushroom bags:

Label each bag
Fill a large pot two thirds full with water and add salt. Warm over medium-high heat, and when hot, add the vegetables and bring to a low simmer. Place mushrooms in a large heatproof bowl and pour in enough hot water to just cover. Let soak until rehydrated and tender, 15 to 20 minutes. Using a big slotted spoon, fish out the mushrooms and place in a large bowl near the stove to keep warm. Set the heat under the pot of water to high and bring to a boil, adding more water if needed to cook the pasta. Cook pasta until al dente. Meanwhile, drizzle the mushrooms with the ghee and smash with the back of the spoon. Grate the cheese and add to the vegetables. When the pasta is done, reserve 1 cup of the cooking water. Drain the pasta and combine with the mushroom mixture. Toss to coat and add back as much of the reserved pasta water as needed to make a lovely sauce. Chop the pistachios, if using, and sprinkle on top of the pasta to serve. Serves 6 to 8.

Spaghetti with Breadcrumbs and Olives, Mushrooms, or Sausage

This tender, flavorful pasta with the crunchy contrast breadcrumbs is a family favorite.

Makes 12 (6 to 8-serving) meals, 4 each of 3 varieties

Ingredients

12 (1-pound) bags spaghetti or other pasta shape

4 cups seasoned dry breadcrumbs

1½ cups plus 1 tablespoon salt, divided

1 tablespoon pepper

4 (½-pint) jars home-canned ground Italian sausage or 4 cups freeze-dried sausage crumbles

4 cups dried mushrooms

4 cups finely grated Parmesan cheese (like Kraft brand)

12 (¼-pint) jars ghee

4 (12-ounce) cans medium black olives

Instructions

For salt: In each of 12 vacuum bags, add and then seal :

- 2 tablespoons salt each (may be combined with pasta)

For breadcrumbs: In each of 12 vacuum bags, add and then seal:

- ⅔ cup dry seasoned dry breadcrumbs
- ¼ teaspoon salt
- ¼ teaspoon pepper

For freeze-dried sausage, if using: In each of 4 vacuum bags, add and then seal:

- 1 dried sausage crumbles

For mushrooms: In each of 4 vacuum bags, add and then seal:

- 1 cup dried mushrooms

For cheese: In each of 12 vacuum bags, add and then seal:

- ½ cup finely grated Parmesan cheese

 Ready-Made Meal Assembly
In each of 8 Mylar bags, tote bags, or vacuum bags, store:

- 1 pound pasta
- 1 bag salt
- 1 bag breadcrumbs
- 1 jar ghee
- 1 can black olives, 1 jar or bag sausage, or 1 bag mushrooms
- 1 bag Parmesan cheese

 Label each bag
Bring a large pot of water to a boil and add the salt. Cook the pasta until al dente, about 8 minutes. If using mushrooms, cover in warm water for 5 minutes, drain and then sauté in half the ghee over medium-high heat until tender. Meanwhile, heat the remaining ghee in a large skillet over medium-high heat, add breadcrumbs and toast until golden. Add the pasta and the mushroom, olives, or sausage to the breadcrumbs and toss to coat. Combine well and serve. Serves 6 to 8.

Tuna Noodle Casserole

This is a classic family favorite, and while not exactly haute cuisine, it's very comforting and homey. I bet you can still remember your mom's tuna casserole. I sure can—it was always what my father answered when she asked him what he wanted for dinner.

Makes 6 (6 to 8-serving) meals

Ingredients

¾ cup salt

6 (1-pound) bags egg noodles, macaroni, or other pasta shape

6 (14.5-ounce) cans cream of chicken or mushroom soup

12 (6-ounce) cans tuna

1½ pounds cheddar cheese, vacuum-sealed into 4-ounce chunks

Instructions

For salt: In each of 6 vacuum bags or zip-top plastic bags, add and then seal:

• 2 tablespoons salt (may be combined with pasta)

Ready-Made Meal Assembly

In each of 6 Mylar bags, tote bags, or vacuum bags, store:

• 1 bag egg noodles, macaroni, or other pasta shape
• 1 packet salt

• 1 can of cream of chicken or mushroom soup
• 2 cans tuna
• 1 packet cheddar cheese

Label each bag

Preheat the oven to 350°F. Bring a large pot of water to a boil and add the salt. Cook the pasta until al dente, about 8 minutes. Meanwhile, in a medium bowl, stir together the soup and 1 can of water. Add the tuna. When the pasta is done, drain, and combine with the soup mixture. Pour out into a 9 x 13-inch pan, grate the cheese on top, and bake 25 to 30 minutes or until bubbly.

Pizza Kits

I think every American family loves pizza. Bake these in the oven or on a grill with the cover on to create an oven effect, or grill them until done on one side, then flip and add toppings and cook until toppings are melted and crust is cooked through.

Makes 16 pizza kits, 4 each in 4 varieties

Ingredients

40 cups flour

⅓ cup sugar

⅓ cup salt

2 cups coconut oil or shortening

16 (.25-ounce) packets active dry yeast

4 (½-pint) jars Home-Canned Beef (page 48) or 8 cups freeze-dried beef or TVP

2 cups dried mushrooms

16 (½-pint) jars Home-Canned Spaghetti Sauce (page 74) or store-bought sauce

16 (4-ounce) vacuum-bags mozzarella cheese or dehydrated mozzarella cheese (½ cup each)

4 (½-pint) jars home-canned sausage or 8 cups freeze-dried sausage crumbles

4 (2.25-ounce) cans sliced black olives

Instructions

For crust mix: In each of 16 vacuum bags, add and then seal:

- 2½ cups flour
- 1 teaspoon sugar
- 1 teaspoon salt
- 1 packet (2 tablespoons) coconut oil or shortening well wrapped in plastic wrap
- 1 packet yeast or 2¼ teaspoons active dry yeast

For freeze-dried meat (if using): In each of 4 vacuum bags, add and then seal:

- 2 cups freeze-dried beef or TVP

For mushrooms: In each of 4 vacuum bags, add and then seal:

- ½ cup dried mushrooms

Ready-Made Meal Assembly

In each of 8 Mylar bags, tote bags, or vacuum bags, store:

- 1 bag crust mix
- 1 can spaghetti sauce
- 1 bag sealed or dehydrated mozzarella cheese
- 1 can/jar/pouch each of ground beef, sausage, olives, or mushrooms

Label each bag
Combine the crust mix with 1 cup of very warm water. Stir to combine and then knead well. Cover and let rise 1 hour or until doubled in size. If using mushrooms, cover with warm water to reconstitute. Preheat the oven to 400°F. Roll out the dough into a large, thin circle. Top with sauce, cheese, and toppings and bake 10 to 15 minutes or until golden. Serves 4 to 6.

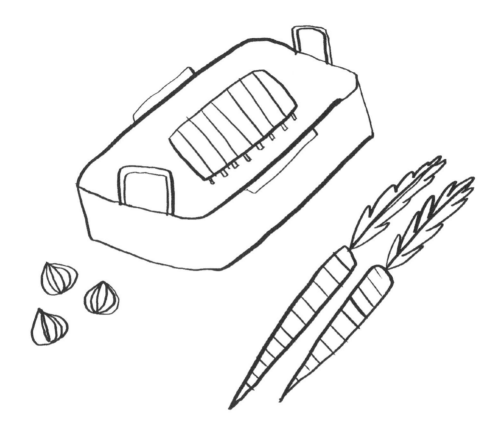

Chapter 7
Ready-Made
Main Course

Chuck Wagon Chili

Chili with beef and beans is truly the classic cowboy food. This version is a sure-fire hit with cowpokes of all ages. I also love it with ground beef instead of beef chunks, and it's especially nice with a combination of both.

Makes 8 (8-serving) meals

Ingredients

8 pounds kidney beans

16 cups dehydrated onion

16 cups dehydrated green bell pepper

½ cup red pepper flakes

1 cup chili powder

½ cup salt

5 tablespoons plus 1 teaspoon black pepper

2 tablespoons plus 2 teaspoons ground cumin

2½ teaspoons cayenne pepper

16 bay leaves

8 pounds Home-Canned Beef (page 48) or 16 cups freeze-dried beef, sausage, or TVP

8 (28-ounce) cans diced tomatoes

Instructions

For beans: In each of 8 vacuum bags, add and then seal:

- 1 pound kidney beans

For chili mix: In each of 8 vacuum bags, add and then seal:

- 2 cups dehydrated onion
- 2 cups dehydrated green bell pepper
- 1 tablespoon red pepper flakes
- 2 tablespoons chili powder
- 1 tablespoon salt

- 2 teaspoons black pepper
- 1 teaspoon ground cumin
- ¼ teaspoon cayenne pepper
- 2 bay leaves
- 2 cups freeze-dried beef or TVP (if using freeze-dried)

For home-canned beef (if using): Pressure-can 8 pints or pint-sized retort pouches for 90 minutes.

Ready-Made Meal Assembly

In each of 8 Mylar bags, tote bags, or vacuum bags, store:

- 1 bag beans
- 1 bag chili mix

- 1 pint beef chunks (if using)
- 1 can tomatoes

Label each bag

Rinse the beans, cover with cold water, and let soak overnight. Drain, transfer to a large soup pot over medium-high heat, and cover with fresh water. Cover and simmer for about 1 hour, or until tender. Add the tomatoes, 6 cups of water, beef, and chili mix. Cover and simmer on low for about 1 hour, adding more water if needed. Serves 8.

Braised Short Ribs

This unctuous braised dish finishes its cooking during the pressure-canning process, which then yields tender beefy ribs and a big-flavored gravy. Pair it with creamy polenta, rice, buttered noodles, or mashed potatoes for a delicious rib-sticking, hearty meal. Make this once and try it, and then come back and make a quadruple batch using a large table-top roaster. You can also cut the meat off the bone after the initial cooking process and before canning to save on jar or retort pouch space.

Makes 1 (6 to 8-serving) meal (about 4 quarts)

Ingredients

8 bone-in short ribs

3 tablespoons olive oil

1 onion, chopped

1½ cups chopped celery

1½ cups chopped carrots

2 cloves garlic, smashed

1 (12-ounce) can tomato paste

2½ cups beef stock or bouillon granules

½ cup grape jelly

2 cups water

1 bunch fresh thyme, wrapped in kitchen twine

2 bay leaves

salt and pepper

Instructions

Preheat the oven to 375°F. Season the short ribs with salt and pepper. In a large skillet over medium-high heat, warm half the oil and brown the ribs very well on all sides. Work in batches if necessary to avoid crowding the pan.

Meanwhile, put the onion, celery, carrots, and garlic in the food processor and process until finely minced. When the meat is fully browned, remove it to a plate and drain off any remaining oil in the pan. Add the remaining oil to the pan and brown the vegetables well. Stir them up and brown them again. Stir in the tomato paste and let brown again. Add the beef stock or bouillon granules and jelly and stir to combine, scraping up any browned bits from the pan. Lower the heat and let the sauce reduce by half.

Add the meat back to the pan and add 2 cups of water, or enough that the sauce nearly covers the meat. Add the thyme and bay leaves. Cover the pan loosely with foil and bake for 90 minutes, turning halfway through the cooking time and adding more water if needed.

Divide the meat in quart-size jars or retort pouches (better because they are flexible) and divide the sauce between them. Seal well and pressure-can for 90 minutes.

Ready-Made Meal Assembly

In a each Mylar bag, tote bag, or vacuum bag, store:

- 1 or 2 quarts short ribs

- 1 sidekit Polenta (page 121), white Rice (page 120), Mashed Potatoes (page 122), or Buttered Noodles (page 120)

Label the bag

Prepare the polenta, rice, mashed potatoes, or buttered noodles according to the package directions. Warm the short ribs in a medium saucepan over medium heat until heated through. Serve over the sidekit. Serves 6 to 8.

Beef Burgundy

Beef burgundy is a classic for good reason—tender beef served in a rich wine sauce is simply delicious.

Makes 16 (6-serving) meals

Ingredients

¼ cup olive oil

16 pounds beef, such as chuck, cubed

3 pounds bacon strips

12 onions, chopped

1 bottle dry red wine, such as burgundy

5 quarts beef stock or ¾ cup beef soup base mixed with 20 cups water

3 (28-ounce) cans diced tomatoes

2 tablespoons sugar

¼ cup dried thyme

16 bay leaves

16 cups dried mushrooms

2 cups all-purpose flour

Instructions

For beef burgundy: In a large pan over medium-high heat, warm the olive oil and brown the beef. In a second large pan, cook the bacon until crisp, reserving the bacon fat. Crumble the bacon and set aside. Cook the onions in the bacon fat until golden. Transfer the onions to a very large stock pot, or divide between 2 large pots. Add the wine, stock, tomatoes, sugar, thyme, and bay leaves. Add the beef and bacon. Simmer for 1 hour. Divide among 16 sterilized quart-size jars or retort pouches, seal, and pressure-can for 90 minutes.

For mushrooms: In each of 16 vacuum bags, add and then seal:

- 1 cup dried mushrooms

For flour: In each of 16 zip-top bags, add and then seal:

- 2 tablespoons flour

Ready-Made Meal Assembly

In each of 16 Mylar bags, tote bags, or vacuum bags, store:

- 1 quart beef burgundy
- 1 bag mushrooms
- 1 bag flour
- 1 sidekit Rice (page 120), Polenta (page 121), Mashed Potatoes (page 122), or Buttered Noodles (page 120)

Label each bag

Prepare the rice, polenta, mashed potatoes, or buttered noodles according to the package directions. Put the mushrooms in a small bowl and add hot water to cover. Let stand for 10 minutes. Heat the beef mixture in a large saucepan over medium-high heat. With a slotted spoon, spoon out the mushrooms and add them to the pot. Stir the flour into ½ cup of the mushroom water and stir into the pot with the beef and mushrooms. Simmer for 15 minutes or until slightly thickened. Serve spooned over the sidekit. Serves 6.

Beef Barbecue

Makes 16 (6 to 8-serving) meals

Ingredients

30 pounds beef roast, such as chuck or brisket

olive oil

7 large onions, chopped

1 cup apple cider vinegar

1 cup lemon juice

5⅔ cups water

15 ribs celery, chopped

1¼ cups Worcestershire sauce

1 cup brown sugar

15 cups ketchup

8 tablespoons prepared yellow mustard

1 cup chili powder

6 teaspoons black pepper

salt

Instructions

Preheat an electric roaster to 350°F or use the oven and 2 large roasting pans. Pat the beef dry and generously season with salt and pepper all over. Preheat one or two skillets over high heat, coat with oil, and brown the beef on all sides. Transfer the beef to the roasting pan(s) and combine the remaining ingredients in a very large bowl to make the sauce. Pour the sauce over the beef and roast for 90 minutes. Cut the beef into large cubes, and use a canning funnel to transfer to 16 sterilized quart-size jars or pouches. Divide the sauce among the jars or pouches, leaving abundant headspace (1 to 2 inches). Wipe the rims or edges to be sealed, add the lids and rims, or heat-seal the pouches. Pressure-can for 90 minutes.

 Ready-Made Meal Assembly
In each of 16 Mylar bags, tote bags, or vacuum bags, store:

- 1 quart beef barbecue

- 1 sidekit Rice (page 120), Polenta (page 121), Mashed Potatoes (page 122), Buttered Noodles (page 120), or Biscuits (page 126)

 Label each bag
Prepare the rice, polenta, mashed potatoes, buttered noodles, or biscuits according to the package directions. Slowly warm the beef barbecue in a pot and serve spooned over the sidekit. Serves 6 to 8.

Saucy Joes

Sloppy yet delicious, Saucy Joes are a family favorite.

Makes 16 (8-serving) meals

Ingredients

16 pounds ground beef

olive oil

16 onions, chopped

8 ribs celery, chopped

7 green bell peppers, chopped

8 cups ketchup

3 (29-ounce) cans tomato sauce

3¾ cups water

1 cup brown sugar, packed

¼ cup dried oregano

salt and pepper

Instructions

Working in batches, brown or boil the beef and drain off the excess oil. Combine the remaining ingredients in a very large bowl to make the sauce. Combine the beef and sauce, and use a canning funnel to transfer the mixture to 16 sterilized quart-size jars or pouches, leaving abundant headspace (1 to 2 inches). Wipe the rims or edges to be sealed, add the lids and rims, or heat-seal the pouches. Pressure-can for 90 minutes.

 Ready-Made Meal Assembly
In each of 16 Mylar bags, tote bags, or vacuum bags, store:

• 1 quart Saucy Joe mix

• 1 sidekit Rice (page 120), Polenta (page 121), Mashed Potatoes (page 122), Buttered Noodles (page 120), Biscuits (page 126), or Dinner Rolls (page 123)

 Label each bag
Prepare the rice, polenta, mashed potatoes, buttered noodles, biscuits, or bread according to the package directions. Slowly warm the saucy joes in a pot and serve spooned over the sidekit. Serves 8.

Spicy Chipotle Beef 4 Ways

This tender braised beef and spicy sauce is big on flavor yet easy on the wallet. We start the braise in the pan and finish it in the canning process.

Makes 12 (6 to 8-serving) meals

Ingredients

20 pounds beef chuck roast, cut into bite-size chunks

olive oil

8 large onions, chopped

3 tablespoons minced garlic

3 (28-ounce) cans diced tomatoes

¼ cup brown sugar, packed

2 (7-ounce) cans chipotle chiles in adobo

salt and pepper

Instructions

Working in batches, chop the beef into chunks, pat dry, and season with salt and pepper. Coat a large skillet with oil over medium-high heat, and brown the beef, working in batches (it needn't be cooked through, just browned). Set aside. Meanwhile, cook the onion in a little oil until it begins to soften. Add the garlic, stir to combine, and then add the tomato sauce and sugar. Puree the chipotle chiles in their sauce in the blender or food processor and add to the sauce. Using a canning funnel, fill the jars or pouches each with 3 cups of beef and then fill with sauce, leaving abundant headspace (1 to 2 inches). Wipe the rims or edges to be sealed, add the lids and rims, or heat-seal the pouches. Pressure-can for 90 minutes.

 Ready-Made Meal Assembly
In each of 12 Mylar bags, tote bags, or vacuum bags, store:

- 1 jar or pouch chipotle beef mix
- 1 sidekit Polenta (page 121), Mashed Potatoes (page 122), Buttered Noodles (page 120), Rice (page 120), or Tortillas (pages 129–30)

 Label each bag
Prepare the polenta, mashed potatoes, buttered noodles, rice, or tortillas according to the package directions. In a large saucepan over medium heat, warm the chipotle beef until heated through. Serve over or alongside the sidekit.

Braised Brisket

This classic dish yields slices of tender beef in a rich, delicious sauce. I use my 18-quart roaster, but your largest roasting pan covered in foil would work in the oven too.

Makes 8 (6-serving) meals

Ingredients

4 (3½ to 4-pound) beef briskets

seasoning salt

3 cups cider vinegar

4 cups tomato paste

1⅓ cups light brown sugar, packed

3 cups finely chopped onions

3 tablespoons minced garlic

Instructions

Preheat a roaster or oven to 325°F. Season the beef with seasoning salt on both sides. In a bowl, stir together the vinegar, tomato paste, brown sugar, onion, and garlic. Pour about half the sauce into the bottom of the pan and lay the briskets over. Top with the remaining sauce. Cover and cook for about 2 hours. Slice the beef against the grain. Using a canning funnel, fill 8 jars or pouches with beef slices and then fill with sauce, leaving abundant headspace (1 to 2 inches). Wipe the rims or edges to be sealed, add the lids and rims, or heat-seal the pouches. Pressure-can for 90 minutes.

 Ready-Made Meal Assembly

In each of 8 Mylar bags, tote bags, or vacuum bags, store:

- 1 jar or pouch brisket and sauce
- 1 sidekit Polenta (page 121), Mashed Potatoes (page 122), Buttered Noodles (page 120), or Rice (page 120)

 Label each bag

Prepare the sidekit according to the package directions. In a large saucepan over medium heat, warm the beef brisket until heated through. Serve over or alongside the sidekit. Serves 6.

Machaca

Depending on which area of Mexico it comes from, spicy braised beef pot roast is either called picadillo or machaca. By any name, it is delicious served with rice, beans, and a side of tortillas. Chuck roast is an excellent choice for this dish, but you can also use whatever roast is on sale.

Makes 16 (8-serving) meals

Ingredients

30 pounds beef roast, such as chuck, cut into ¼-pound chunks

seasoning salt

vegetable oil

7 large onions, chopped

4 cups water

2 (28-ounce) cans green enchilada sauce

Instructions

Preheat an electric roaster to 325°F or use the oven and 2 large roasting pans or slow cookers set on high. Pat the beef chunks dry and generously season with seasoning salt all over. Preheat 1 or 2 skillets over high heat, coat with oil, and brown the beef on all sides. Transfer the beef to the roasting pan(s) and add the onion, water, and enchilada sauce. Cover and cook the beef for 3 hours. Using a canning funnel, add the beef to 16 sterilized quart-size jars or pouches and divide the sauce among the pouches, leaving abundant headspace (1 to 2 inches). Wipe the rims or edges to be sealed, add the lids and rims, or heat-seal the pouches. Pressure-can for 90 minutes.

 Ready-Made Meal Assembly
In each of 16 Mylar bags, tote bags, or vacuum bags, store:

- 1 quart beef machaca

- 1 sidekit Rice (page 120), Polenta (page 121), Mashed Potatoes (page 122), Buttered Noodles (page 120), Corn Tortillas (page 130), or Flour Tortillas (page 129)

 Label each bag
Prepare the rice, polenta, mashed potatoes, noodles, or tortillas according to the package directions. Slowly warm the beef machaca in a pot, shred with a fork, and serve spooned over the sidekit. Serves 8.

Beef and Vegetables 12 Ways

It's amazing how many recipes start out with browned beef, onions, carrots, and celery and have some beef stock in them. We'll can this very simple base and add a variety of extra ingredients and sidekits to make all different kinds of meals. Chuck is best for these recipes, but go with what looks best to you when you're shopping or what is on sale.

Makes 16 (8-serving) meals

Ingredients

16 pounds beef roast, such as chuck

olive oil

2 cups beef soup base or bouillon granules, divided

24 cups (6 quarts) water

16 onions, chopped

12 ribs celery, chopped

12 carrots, peeled and chopped

4 cups butter-flavored vegetable shortening or 4 cups ghee packaged in quarter-pint jars or pouches

4 cups flour

5⅓ cups dry milk

salt and pepper

Instructions

For beef stew mix: Working in batches, chop beef into chunks, season with salt and pepper, and brown the beef in olive oil on all sides (it needn't be cooked through, just browned). In a large bowl, mix 1 cup of the soup base with the water. Adjust the seasoning to taste. Stir to scrape up any browned bits from the bottom of the pan and add it back into the soup mixture. Using a canning funnel, fill 16 sterilized quart-size jars or pouches each with 2 cups beef, 1 cup onions, and ¾ cup each celery and carrots. Fill with soup base liquid, leaving abundant headspace (1 to 2 inches). Wipe the rims or edges to be sealed, add the lids and rims, or heat-seal the pouches. Pressure-can for 90 minutes.

For thickener: In each of 16 vacuum bags, add and seal:

- ¼ cup butter-flavored vegetable shortening or one ¼-pint ghee
- ¼ cup flour in a zip-top bag

For gravy mix: In each of 16 vacuum bags, add and seal:

- ⅓ cup dry milk
- 1 tablespoon beef soup base or bouillon granules

Beef Stew Ready-Made Meal Assembly (serves 4)

In each of 16 Mylar bags, tote bags, or vacuum bags, store:

- 1 jar or pouch beef stew mix
- 1 packet thickener
- 1 packet gravy mix

Label each bag
In a large saucepan, melt together the flour and shortening or ghee from the thickener packet, and stir and cook for 3 minutes to make a roux. Open the beef and the drain liquid into a 4-cup measuring cup or bowl. Stir in the gravy mix and enough water to equal about 4 cups. Add the gravy mix liquid to the roux. Over medium-high heat, stir and cook until thickened. Stir in the beef and vegetables, and cook until heated through. Serves 4.

Beef Pot Pie Ready-Made Meal Assembly (serves 8)

In each of 16 Mylar bags, tote bags, or vacuum bags, store:

- 1 jar or pouch beef stew mix
- 1 packet thickener
- 1 packet gravy mix
- 1 Pie Crust Sidekit (page 127)

Label each bag

Preheat the oven to 350°F. In a large saucepan over medium heat, melt together the flour and shortening or ghee from the thickener packet, and stir and cook for 3 minutes to make a roux. Open the beef and drain the liquid into a 4-cup measuring cup or bowl. Stir in the gravy mix and enough water to equal 4 cups. Add the gravy mix liquid to the roux. Over medium-high heat, stir and cook until thickened. Stir in the beef and vegetables, cook until heated through, and remove from the heat. Prepare the pie crust according to the package directions. Transfer the filling to one 9 x 13-inch baking dish or multiple smaller dishes. Roll out the pie crust and use it to top the filling. Bake for 30 to 35 minutes, until golden. Let stand 10 minutes before serving. Serves 8.

Shepherd's Pie Ready-Made Meal Assembly (serves 8)

In each of 16 Mylar bags, tote bags, or vacuum bags, store:

- 1 jar or pouch beef stew mix
- 1 packet thickener
- 1 packet gravy mix
- 1 sidekit Mashed Potatoes (page 122)
- 1 vacuum packet containing ½ cup finely grated Parmesan cheese and 1 tablespoon garlic powder

Label each bag

Preheat the oven to 350°F. In a large saucepan over medium heat, melt together the flour and shortening or ghee from the thickener packet, and stir and cook for 3 minutes to make a roux. Open the beef and drain the liquid into a 4-cup measuring cup or bowl. Stir in the gravy mix and enough water to equal 4 cups. Add the gravy mix liquid to the roux. Over medium-high heat, stir and cook until thickened. Stir in the beef and vegetables, cook until heated through, and remove from the heat. Prepare the mashed potatoes according to the package directions, and stir in the garlic-Parmesan mixture. Transfer the filling to one 9 x 13-inch baking dish or multiple smaller dishes, and top with the mashed potatoes, spreading to cover. Bake 30 to 45 minutes, until golden. Let stand 10 minutes before serving. Serves 8.

Beef Noodle Soup Ready-Made Meal Assembly (serves 8)

In each of 16 Mylar bags, tote bags, or vacuum bags, store:

- 1 jar or pouch beef stew mix
- 1 vacuum bag containing 3 cups egg noodles and ¼ cup beef soup base

Label each bag

In a large soup pot, combine all the ingredients plus 12 cups of water. Bring to a boil, reduce to a simmer, and cook for about 8 minutes, until the beef is heated through and the noodles are tender. Serves 8.

Beef Pot Pie with Cheddar Cheese Crust Ready-Made Meal Assembly (serves 8)

In each of 16 Mylar bags, tote bags, or vacuum bags, seal:

- 1 jar or pouch beef stew mix
- 1 packet thickener
- 1 packet gravy
- 1 bag Cheddar Cheese Crust (page 127)

Label each bag

Preheat the oven to 350°F. In a large saucepan over medium heat, melt together the flour and shortening or ghee from the thickener packet, and stir and cook for 3 minutes to make a roux. Open the beef and drain the liquid into a 4-cup measuring cup or bowl. Stir in the gravy mix and enough water to equal 4 cups. Add the gravy mix liquid to the roux. Over medium-high heat, stir and cook until thickened. Stir in the beef and vegetables, cook until heated through, and remove from the heat. Prepare the cheddar cheese crust according to the package directions. Transfer the beef filling to one 9 x 13-inch baking dish or multiple smaller dishes. Roll out the pie crust and use it to top the filling. Bake for 30 to 35 minutes, until golden. Let stand 10 minutes before serving. Serves 8.

Beefy Noodle Casserole Ready-Made Meal Assembly (serves 8)

In each of 16 Mylar bags, tote bags, or vacuum bags, seal:

- 1 jar or pouch beef stew mix
- 1 vacuum bag containing 1½ cups dehydrated mushrooms or peas
- 1 packet thickener
- 1 packet gravy mix
- 1 vacuum bag containing 3 cups egg noodles and 1 tablespoon salt

Label each bag

Preheat the oven to 350°F. Bring a large pot of water to boil for the noodles. Add the noodles, salt, and mushrooms or peas, and cook about 8 minutes. Drain and reserve. Meanwhile, in a large saucepan over medium heat, melt together the flour and shortening or ghee from the thickener packet, and stir and cook for 3 minutes to make a roux. Open the beef and drain the liquid into a 4-cup measuring cup or bowl. Stir in the gravy mix and enough water to equal 4 cups. Add the gravy mix liquid to the roux. Over medium-high heat, stir and cook until thickened. Stir in the beef and vegetables, cook until heated through, and remove from heat. Mix the noodles and beef mix together. Serve as is, or pour into a 9 x 13-inch baking dish and bake for 25 to 30 minutes, until bubbly. Let stand for 10 minutes before serving. Serves 8.

Saucy Beef and Vegetables with Polenta, Mashed Potatoes, Rice, or Biscuits Ready-Made Meal Assembly (serves 8)

In each of 16 Mylar bags, tote bags, or vacuum bags, store:

- 1 jar or pouch beef stew mix
- 1 packet thickener
- 1 packet gravy mix

- 1 sidekit Polenta (page 121), Mashed Potatoes (page 122), Rice (page 120), Biscuits (page 126), or Naan Bread (page 131)

Label each bag

Prepare the sidekit according to the package directions. Meanwhile, in a large saucepan over medium heat, melt together the flour and shortening or ghee from the thickener packet, and stir and cook for 3 minutes to make a roux. Open the beef and drain the liquid into a 4-cup measuring cup or bowl. Stir in the gravy mix and enough water to equal 4 cups. Add the gravy mix liquid to the roux. Over medium-high heat, stir and cook until thickened. Stir in the beef and vegetables, and cook until heated through. Serve on top of or alongside the sidekit. Serves 8.

Best Ever Baby Back Ribs

This recipe is easy and yields hugely flavored ribs and a delicious barbecue sauce.

Makes 4 (6 to 8-serving) quarts

Ingredients

4 racks baby back ribs

seasoning salt

water, as needed

2 cups prepared barbecue sauce

pork drippings plus water to make 2 cups

Instructions

Preheat the oven to 350°F. Generously season the ribs with seasoning salt, wrap well in foil, and bake for 1½ hours on 2 rimmed baking sheets. Let cool for 10 minutes. Carefully unwrap the ribs, reserving any juices. Cut between the bones and pack the ribs in canning jars or retort pouches. Add water to the reserved juices to make 2 cups total, and add in the 2 cups of barbecue sauce. Divide the ribs among 4 quart-size jars or retort pouches and add the sauce, dividing it up between the jars or pouches. Seal the jars or pouches and pressure-can for 90 minutes.

Ready-Made Meal Assembly

In Mylar bags, tote bags, or vacuum bags, store:

- 1 or 2 quarts ribs

- 1 sidekit Polenta (page 121), White Rice (page 120), Mashed Potatoes (page 122), or Buttered Noodles (page 120)

Label each bag

Prepare the polenta, white rice, mashed potatoes, or buttered noodles according to the package directions. Heat the ribs on a hot grill, basting with sauce, for about 10 minutes or until heated through. Serve alongside the sidekit. Serves 6 to 8.

Pulled Pork

Pulled pork is my go-to recipe for entertaining a crowd in the summertime. It basically cooks itself. Just season it and slow-cook it low and slow until it is fall-off-the-bone tender. I use an 18-quart Nesco roaster oven, which is a table top, plug-in appliance with a large roasting pan and lid. It is meant for slow, moist cooking and it renders the pork incredibly tender and flavorful. We cook it here with ingredients that cook up into a barbecue sauce, or you can use commercially prepared barbecue sauce thinned with water.

Makes 16 (6 to 8-serving) meals

Ingredients

30 pounds pork (about 2 whole pork shoulders)

7 large onions, chopped

1 cup apple cider vinegar

1 cup lemon juice

5⅔ cups water

15 ribs celery, chopped

1¼ cups Worcestershire sauce

1 cup brown sugar, packed

15 cups ketchup

½ cup prepared mustard

1 cup chili powder

6 teaspoons black pepper

salt

Instructions

Preheat an electric roaster to 350°F or use the oven and 2 large roasting pans or slow cookers set on high. Pat the pork dry and generously season with salt and pepper all over. Preheat one or two skillets over high heat, coat with oil, and brown the pork on all sides. Add the pork to the roasting pan(s) and combine the remaining ingredients in a very large bowl to make the sauce. Pour the sauce over the pork and roast for 4 hours. Cut the pork into large cubes, and use a canning funnel to add the pork to 16 sterilized quart-size jars or pouches. Divide the sauce among the jars or pouches, leaving abundant headspace (1 to 2 inches). Wipe the rims or edges to be sealed, add the lids and rims, or heat-seal the pouches. Pressure-can for 90 minutes.

 Ready-Made Meal Assembly

In each of 16 Mylar bags, tote bags, or vacuum bags, store:

- 1 quart pulled pork

- 1 sidekit Rice (page 120), Polenta (page 121), Mashed Potatoes (page 122), Buttered Noodles (page 120), or Biscuits (page 126)

 Label each bag
Slowly warm the pork in a pot. Shred with a fork, and serve spooned over the sidekit. Serves 6 to 8.

Carnitas

Carnitas are a beautiful Mexican braised pork dish traditionally served with tortillas. I love carnitas over rice best, because the rice soaks up the delicious sauce.

Makes 16 (8-serving) meals

Ingredients

30 pounds pork (about 2 whole pork shoulders)

oil

7 large onions, chopped

4 cups water

2 (28-ounce) cans green enchilada sauce

salt and pepper

Instructions

Preheat an electric roaster to 325°F or use the oven and 2 large roasting pans or slow cookers set on high. Pat the pork dry and generously season with salt and pepper all over. Preheat one or two skillets over high heat, coat with oil, and brown the pork on all sides. Transfer the pork to the roasting pan(s) and add the onion, water, and enchilada sauce. Cook the pork for 4 hours. Cut the pork into large cubes, and use a canning funnel to add the pork to 16 sterilized quart-size jars or pouches. Divide the sauce among the pouches, leaving abundant headspace (1 to 2 inches). Wipe the rims or edges to be sealed, add the lids and rims, or heat-seal the pouches. Pressure-can for 90 minutes.

Ready-Made Meal Assembly

In each of 16 Mylar bags, tote bags, or vacuum bags, store:

- 1 quart carnitas

- 1 sidekit Rice (page 120), Polenta (page 121), Mashed Potatoes (page 122), Buttered Noodles (page 120), Corn Tortillas (page 130), or Flour Tortillas (page 129)

Label each bag

Prepare the rice, polenta, mashed potatoes, buttered noodles, or tortillas according to the package directions. Slowly warm the carnitas in a pot and serve spooned over the sidekit. Serves 8.

Spicy Braised Pork

My favorite way to eat this tender pork is over cheesy grits, the perfect balance for the spicy sauce.

Makes 12 (6 to 8-serving) bags

Ingredients

20 pounds pork shoulder roast

8 large onions, chopped

2 tablespoons olive oil

3 tablespoons minced garlic

3 (28-ounce) cans diced tomatoes

¼ cup brown sugar, packed

2 (7-ounce) cans chipotle chiles in adobo

salt and pepper

Instructions

Preheat an electric roaster to 325°F or use the oven and 2 large roasting pans or slow cookers set on high. Pat the pork dry, season with salt and pepper and cook, covered for about 4 hours with 2 inches of water in the bottom of the roasting pan. Meanwhile make the sauce: Cook the onion in the oil until it begins to soften. Add the garlic, stir to combine, and then add the tomato sauce and sugar. Puree the chipotles in their sauce a the blender or food processor and add to the sauce. When the pork is tender, cut it into chunks. Using a canning funnel, fill 12 sterilized quart-size jars or pouches each with 3 cups of pork and then fill with sauce, leaving abundant headspace (1 to 2 inches). Wipe the rims or edges to be sealed, add the lids and rims, or heat-seal the pouches. Pressure-can for 90 minutes.

 Ready-Made Meal Assembly
In each of 12 Mylar bags, vacuum bags, or tote bags, store:

• 1 jar or pouch braised pork

• 1 sidekit Polenta (page 121), Mashed Potatoes (page 122), Buttered Noodles (page 120), Rice (page 120), Naan Bread (page 131), or Biscuits (page 126)

 Label each bag
Prepare the polenta, mashed potatoes, buttered noodles, rice, or biscuits according to the package directions. In a large saucepan over medium heat, warm the spicy braised pork until heated through. Serve over or alongside the sidekit. Serves 6 to 8.

Tamarind-Braised Pulled Pork

This recipe is one I make when I'm entertaining, and people practically lick the plates. This tangy barbecue sauce is divine. It has a sweet and spicy kick to it. Tamarind pulp is used frequently in Asian and Latin cooking. It's the primary ingredient in Worcestershire sauce, so you will recognize the flavor. If your grocery store doesn't carry it in the international foods section, you can easily order it online.

Makes 8 (6 to 8-serving) meals

Ingredients

4 cups light brown sugar, packed

3½ cups seedless tamarind paste

1 cup grated fresh ginger

1 cup chopped fresh oregano

¼ cup ground coriander

2½ tablespoons salt

1½ tablespoons red pepper flakes

24 cups (6 quarts) water

4 pork shoulders (about 24 pounds total)

salt and pepper

vegetable oil

Instructions

Preheat an 18-quart roaster oven to 350°F. In a large pot over medium-high heat, combine all the ingredients except the pork, salt, pepper, and oil, and simmer for about 10 minutes. Coat a large skillet with oil, cut the pork into large chunks, salt and pepper it, and brown it on all sides over medium-high heat. Add the pork to the roaster and pour the sauce over. Cook for 60 minutes. Using a canning funnel, fill 8 sterilized quart-size jars or pouches each with pork and sauce, leaving abundant headspace (1 to 2 inches). Wipe the rims or edges to be sealed, add the lids and rims, or heat-seal the pouches. Pressure-can for 90 minutes.

 Ready-Made Meal Assembly
In each of 8 Mylar bags, tote bags, or vacuum bags, store:

- 1 jar or pouch pulled pork

- 1 sidekit Polenta (page 121), Mashed Potatoes (page 122), Buttered Noodles (page 120), or Rice (page 120)

 Label each bag
Prepare the polenta, mashed potatoes, buttered noodles, or rice according to the package directions. In a large saucepan over medium heat, warm the braised pork until heated through. Serve over or alongside the sidekit. Serves 6 to 8.

Braised Country-Style Ribs 4 Ways

Country-style ribs are meaty pork ribs that can be bought either on or off the bone. I prefer cooking them on the bone because the flavor is fantastic, but there is also something to be said for being able to fit more meat in each packet, so I leave the choice up to you. Both ways, it is delicious.

Makes 12 (6 to 8-serving) meals

Ingredients

¼ cup olive oil, plus more as needed

22 pounds country ribs

salt and pepper

8 large onions, chopped

8 carrots, chopped

8 ribs celery, chopped

½ cup minced garlic

½ cup tomato paste

2 cups apple cider vinegar

2½ tablespoons red pepper flakes

10 bay leaves

20 cups (5 quarts) chicken stock or prepared soup base

Instructions

Preheat an 18-quart roaster oven to 350°F. Warm 2 tablespoons oil in a large skillet over medium-high heat. Season the pork with salt and pepper, and brown in batches, adding more oil as needed. Meanwhile to make the sauce, warm 2 tablespoons oil in a large saucepan over medium-high heat. Cook the onion, carrots, and celery until they begin to soften. Add the garlic, stir to combine, and then add the tomato paste, vinegar, and red pepper flakes. Add the bay leaves and chicken stock and simmer for about 10 minutes. Add the pork to the roaster and cover with sauce. Cook for 1 hour. Using a canning funnel, fill 12 sterilized quart-size jars or pouches each with pork and then fill with sauce, leaving abundant headspace (1 to 2 inches). Wipe the rims or edges to be sealed, add the lids and rims, or heat-seal the pouches. Pressure-can for 90 minutes.

 ### Ready-Made Meal Assembly
In each of 12 Mylar bags, vacuum bags, or tote bags, store:

- 1 jar or pouch braised ribs
- 1 sidekit Polenta (page 121), Mashed Potatoes (page 122), Buttered Noodles (page 120), or Rice (page 120)

 ### Label each bag
Prepare the polenta, mashed potatoes, buttered noodles, or rice according to package directions. In a large saucepan over medium heat, warm the braised ribs until heated through. Serve over or alongside the sidekit. Serves 6 to 8.

Tamarind-Braised Pork Ribs

This tamarind-based barbecue sauce is beyond delicious. It has a slightly Asian flair, sweet heat, and delicious tanginess. I use baby back ribs for this recipe, but this would be delicious on any style of ribs.

Makes 8 (6 to 8-serving) meals

Ingredients

4 cups light brown sugar, packed

3½ cups seedless tamarind paste

1 cup grated fresh ginger

1 cup chopped fresh oregano

¼ cup ground coriander

2½ tablespoons salt

1½ tablespoons red pepper flakes

24 cups (6 quarts) water

8 racks baby back pork ribs (about 32 pounds total)

Instructions

Preheat an 18-quart roaster over to 350°F. In a large pot, add all the ingredients except the ribs and simmer for about 10 minutes. Add the ribs to the roaster and coat with the sauce. Cook for 45 minutes. Cut the ribs apart and coat in the sauce again. Using a canning funnel, fill 8 sterilized quart-size jars or pouches each with ribs and sauce, leaving abundant headspace (1 to 2 inches). Wipe the rims or edges to be sealed, add the lids and rims, or heat-seal the pouches. Pressure-can for 90 minutes.

 Ready-Made Meal Assembly
In each of 8 Mylar bags, vacuum bags, or tote bags, store:

• 1 jar or pouch ribs

• 1 sidekit Polenta (page 121), Mashed Potatoes (page 122), Buttered Noodles (page 120), or Rice (page 120)

 Label each bag
Prepare the polenta, mashed potatoes, buttered noodles, or rice according to the package directions. In a large saucepan over medium heat or on a grill, warm the braised ribs until heated through. Spoon on any extra sauce and serve over or alongside the sidekit. Serves 6 to 8.

Braised Chicken and Mushrooms

This recipe creates delicious, rich tomato gravy for tender chicken and earthy mushrooms.

Makes 12 (6 to 8-servings) meals

Ingredients

24 pounds boneless, skinless chicken thighs

olive oil

8 large onions, chopped

12 pounds button mushrooms, thinly sliced

½ cup minced garlic

1½ cups tomato paste

1 tablespoon paprika

1 teaspoon cayenne pepper

1½ cups flour

24 cups (6 quarts) chicken stock or prepared soup base

1½ cups chopped fresh rosemary

salt and pepper

Instructions

Season the chicken with salt and pepper. Coat a large skillet with oil and warm over medium-high heat. Brown the chicken in batches, adding more oil as needed. Meanwhile make the sauce: Coat a large skillet with oil and warm over medium-high heat. Cook the onion and mushrooms until they begin to soften. Add the garlic, stir to combine, and then add the tomato paste, paprika, and cayenne. Sprinkle in the flour and stir well to combine. Cook for 5 minutes. Add the chicken stock and rosemary and simmer for about 10 minutes. Using a canning funnel, fill 12 sterilized quart-size jars or pouches each with chicken and then fill with sauce, leaving abundant headspace (1 to 2 inches). Wipe the rims or edges to be sealed, add the lids and rims, or heat-seal the pouches. Pressure-can for 90 minutes.

 Ready-Made Meal Assembly

In each of 12 Mylar bags, vacuum bags, or tote bags, store:

- 1 jar or pouch chicken and mushrooms

- 1 sidekit Polenta (page 121), Mashed Potatoes (page 122), Buttered Noodles (page 120), or Rice (page 120)

 Label each bag
Prepare the polenta, mashed potatoes, buttered noodles, or rice according to the package directions. In a large saucepan over medium heat, warm the chicken and mushrooms until heated through. Serve over or alongside the sidekit. Serves 6 to 8.

Braised Chicken Legs and Thighs in Tomato Sauce

These chicken thighs have great depth of flavor, and you'll want to sop up all the sauce with the sidekit you serve it with.

Makes 12 (6 to 8-serving) meals

Ingredients

24 pounds chicken legs and thighs

salt and pepper

olive oil

1 tablespoon paprika

1 teaspoon whole cumin seeds

2 teaspoons red pepper flakes

8 large white onions, peeled, halved, and thinly sliced

1 cup grated fresh ginger

1 cup halved garlic cloves

8 (28-ounce) cans whole, peeled tomatoes

4 cinnamon sticks

4 fresh or dried bay leaves

water, as needed

Instructions

Season the chicken with salt and pepper. Coat a large skillet with oil and warm over medium-high heat. Brown the chicken in batches, adding more oil as needed. Meanwhile, make the sauce: Coat a large skillet with oil and warm over medium-high heat. Cook the paprika, cumin seeds, red pepper flakes, and onion until it begins to soften. Add the ginger and garlic, stir to combine, and then add the tomatoes. Add the cinnamon sticks and bay leaves and cook for 20 minutes. Using a canning funnel, fill 12 sterilized quart-size jars or pouches each with chicken and then with sauce, leaving abundant headspace (1 to 2 inches). Wipe the rims or edges to be sealed, add the lids and rims, or heat-seal the pouches. Pressure-can for 90 minutes.

 Ready-Made Meal Assembly

In each of 12 Mylar bags, vacuum bags, or tote bags, store:

- 1 jar or pouch chicken in tomato sauce
- 1 sidekit Polenta (page 121), Mashed Potatoes (page 122), Buttered Noodles (page 120), or Rice (page 120)

 Label each bag

Prepare the polenta, mashed potatoes, buttered noodles, or rice according to package directions. In a large saucepan over medium heat, warm the spicy braised chicken until heated through. Serve over or with sidekit. Serves 6 to 8.

Classic Chicken and Vegetables 10 Ways

Did you ever notice how many recipes start with chicken, onion, celery, and carrots in chicken stock? You can go dozens of ways with this flexible beginning. Our approach here is to create a great flavor base by partially browning the chicken to start. Be sure to taste your chicken stock and make sure it has great flavor, but isn't too salty. Once we've canned the chicken and vegetables, we can thicken the chicken stock with a butter and flour roux to make a creamy gravy. This is delicious served over biscuits, or tucked into a flakey pie crust for chicken pot pie, or simmered with oh-so-tender dumplings. This recipe, more than any other, tastes like home to me.

Makes 16 (8-serving) meals, in 12 different varieties

Ingredients

16 pounds boneless, skinless chicken thighs (or breasts)

olive oil

salt and pepper

2 cups chicken soup base or bouillon granules, divided

24 cups (6 quarts) of water

16 onions, chopped

12 ribs celery, chopped

12 carrots, peeled and chopped

4 cups butter-flavored vegetable shortening or 4 cups ghee packaged in quarter-pint jars or pouches

4 cups flour

5⅓ cups dry milk

Instructions

For chicken stew mix: Working in batches, chop the chicken into chunks and season with salt and pepper. Coat a large skillet with oil and brown the chicken on all sides (it needn't be cooked through, just browned). Mix the soup base or bouillon and the water. Adjust the seasoning to taste. Stir to scrape up any browned bits from the bottom of the pan, and add them back into the soup mixture. Using a canning funnel, fill 16 sterilized quart-size jars or pouches each with 2 cups of chicken, 1 cup onions, and ¾ cup each of celery and carrots. Fill with soup base liquid, leaving abundant headspace (1 to 2 inches). Wipe the rims or edges to be sealed, add the lids and rims, or heat-seal the pouches. Pressure-can for 90 minutes.

For thickener: In each of 16 vacuum bags, add and then seal:

- ¼ cup butter-flavored vegetable shortening or one ¼-pint ghee
- ¼ cup flour in a zip-top bag

For gravy mix: In each of 16 vacuum bags, add and then seal:

- ⅓ cup dry milk
- 1 tablespoon chicken soup base or bouillon granules

Chicken and Dumplings Ready-Made Meal Assembly (serves 8)

In each of 16 Mylar bags, tote bags, or vacuum bags, store:

- 1 jar or pouch chicken stew mix
- 1 packet thickener
- 1 packet gravy
- 1 sidekit Biscuit Mix (page 126)

Label each bag

In a large saucepan, melt together the flour and shortening or ghee from the thickener packet, and stir and cook for 3 minutes to make a roux. Open the chicken and drain the liquid into a 4-cup measuring cup or bowl. Stir in the gravy mix and enough water to equal about 4 cups. Add the gravy mix liquid to the roux. Over medium-high heat, stir and cook until thickened. Stir in the chicken and vegetables, and cook until heated through. Meanwhile, mix the biscuit dough, but instead of baking as directed, roll out the dough until ¼ inch thick, then cut into 1-inch squares. Drop the squares into the chicken mixture, press gently and quickly to submerge, and cover tightly to steam the dumplings. Cook for about 10 minutes and taste a dumpling to be sure it is cooked through. If it is, serve; if not cook 5 minutes more. Serves 8.

Chicken Pot Pie Ready-Made Meal Assembly (serves 8)

In each of 16 Mylar bags, tote bags, or vacuum bags, store:

- 1 jar or pouch chicken stew mix
- 1 packet thickener
- 1 packet gravy mix
- 1 Pie Crust Sidekit (page 127)

Label each bag

Preheat the oven to 350°F. In a large saucepan, melt together the flour and shortening or ghee from the thickener packet, and stir and cook for 3 minutes to make a roux. Open the chicken and drain the liquid into a 4-cup measuring cup or bowl. Stir in the gravy mix and enough water to equal 4 cups. Add the gravy mix liquid to the roux. Over medium-high heat, stir and cook until thickened. Stir in the chicken and vegetables, and cook until heated through. Remove from the heat. Prepare the pie crust according to the package directions. Transfer the chicken filling to one 9 x 13-inch baking dish or multiple smaller dishes. Roll out the pie crust and use it to top the dish. Bake for 30 to 35 minutes, until golden, and let stand for 10 minutes before serving. Serves 8.

Chicken Shepherd's Pie Ready-Made Meal Assembly (serves 8)

In each of 16 Mylar bags, tote bags, or vacuum bags, store:

- 1 jar or pouch chicken stew mix
- 1 packet thickener
- 1 packet gravy mix
- 1 sidekit Mashed Potatoes (page 122)
- 1 vacuum bag containing ½ cup finely grated Parmesan cheese and 1 tablespoon garlic powder

Label each bag

Preheat the oven to 350°F. In a large saucepan over medium heat, melt together the flour and shortening or ghee from the thickener packet, and stir and cook for 3 minutes to make a roux. Open the chicken and drain the liquid into a 4-cup measuring cup or bowl. Stir in the gravy mix and enough water to equal 4 cups. Add the gravy mix liquid to the roux. Over medium-high heat, stir and cook until thickened. Stir in the chicken and vegetables, and cook until heated through. Remove from the heat. Prepare the mashed potatoes according to the package directions and stir in the garlic-Parmesan mixture. Transfer the filling to one 9 x 13-inch baking dish or multiple smaller dishes, and top with mashed potato, spreading to cover. Bake for 30 to 45 minutes, until golden, and let stand for 10 minutes before serving. Serves 8.

Chicken Noodle Soup Ready-Made Meal Assembly (serves 8)

In each of 16 Mylar bags, tote bags, or vacuum bags, store:

- 1 jar or pouch chicken stew mix
- 1 vacuum bag containing 3 cups egg noodles and ¼ cup chicken soup base

Label each bag

In a large soup pot, combine all the ingredients plus 12 cups of water. Bring to a boil over high heat, reduce the heat to a simmer, and cook for about 8 minutes or until chicken is heated through and noodles are tender. Serves 8.

Chicken and Rice Soup Ready-Made Meal Assembly (serves 8)

In each of 16 Mylar bags, tote bags, or vacuum bags, store:

- 1 jar or pouch chicken stew mix
- 1 vacuum bag containing 2 cups rice and ¼ cup chicken soup base

Label each bag

In a large soup pot, combine all the ingredients plus 12 cups of water. Bring to a boil over high heat, reduce to a simmer and cook for about 20 minutes or until the chicken is heated through and the rice is done. Serves 8.

Chicken Noodle Casserole Ready-Made Meal Assembly (serves 8)

In each of 16 Mylar bags, tote bags, or vacuum bags, store:

- 1 vacuum packet 1½ cups dried mushrooms
- 1 packet thickener
- 1 packet gravy mix
- 1 vacuum bag containing 3 cups egg noodles and 1 tablespoon salt

Label each bag

Preheat the oven to 350°F. Bring a large pot of water to boil over high heat. Add the noodles, mushrooms, and salt, and cook for about 8 minutes, until noodles are tender. Drain and reserve. Meanwhile, in a large saucepan over medium heat, melt together the flour and shortening or ghee from the thickener packet, and stir and cook for 3 minutes. Open the chicken and drain the liquid into a 4-cup measuring cup or bowl. Stir in the gravy mix and enough water to equal 4 cups. Add the gravy mix liquid to the roux. Over medium-high heat, stir and cook until thickened. Stir in the chicken and vegetables, and cook until heated through. Remove from the heat. Stir the noodles and chicken stew mix together. You may serve as is or pour into a 9 x 13-inch baking dish and bake for 25 to 30 minutes, until bubbly. Let stand for 10 minutes before serving. Serves 8.

Chicken Noodle Casserole with Crunchy Breadcrumb Topping Ready-Made Meal Assembly (serves 8)

In each of 16 Mylar bags, tote bags, or vacuum bags, store:

- 1 jar or pouch chicken stew mix
- 1 vacuum bag containing 1½ cups dried peas
- 1 packet thickener
- 1 packet gravy mix
- 1 vacuum bag containing 3 cups egg noodles and 1 tablespoon salt
- 1 vacuum bag containing ¾ cup breadcrumbs and ¼ cup finely grated Parmesan cheese

Label each bag

Preheat the oven to 350°F. Bring a large pot of water to boil over high heat. Add noodles, peas, and salt, and cook for about 8 minutes, until noodles are tender. Drain and reserve. Meanwhile, in a large saucepan over medium heat, melt together the flour and shortening or ghee from the thickener packet, and stir and cook for 3 minutes to make a roux. Open the chicken and drain the liquid into a 4-cup measuring cup or bowl. Stir in the gravy mix and enough water to equal 4 cups. Add the gravy mix liquid to the roux. Over medium-high heat, stir and cook until thickened. Stir in the chicken and vegetables, and cook until heated through. Remove from the heat. Mix the noodles and chicken stew mix together. Pour into a 9 x 13-inch baking dish, top with the breadcrumb-Parmesan mixture, and bake for 25 to 30 minutes, until bubbly. Let stand for 10 minutes before serving. Serves 8.

Chicken Divan Ready-Made Meal Assembly (serves 8)

In each of 16 Mylar bags, tote bags, or vacuum bags, store:

- 1 jar or pouch chicken stew mix
- 1 vacuum bag containing 2 cups dehydrated broccoli
- 1 bag thickener
- 1 bag gravy mix
- 1 vacuum bag containing 3 cups egg noodles and 1 tablespoon salt

Label each bag

Preheat the oven to 350°F. Bring a large pot of water to boil over high heat. Add the broccoli and cook for 8 minutes. Add the noodles and salt and cook about 8 minutes more. Drain and reserve. Meanwhile, in a large saucepan over medium heat, melt together the flour and shortening or ghee from the thickener packet, and stir and cook for 3 minutes to make a roux. Open the chicken and drain the liquid into a 4-cup measuring cup or bowl. Stir in the gravy mix and enough water to equal 4 cups. Add the gravy mix liquid to the roux. Over medium-high heat, stir and cook until thickened. Stir in the chicken stew mix, cook until heated through, and remove from the heat. Mix the noodles and chicken stew mix together. You may serve as is or pour into a 9 x 13-inch baking dish and bake for 25 to 30 minutes, until bubbly. Let stand for 10 minutes before serving. Serves 8.

Chicken, Broccoli, and Rice Casserole Ready-Made Meal Assembly (serves 8)

In each of 16 Mylar bags, tote bags, or vacuum bags, store:

- 1 jar or pouch chicken stew mix
- 1 vacuum bag containing 2 cups dehydrated broccoli
- 1 bag thickener
- 1 bag gravy mix
- 1 vacuum bag containing 2 cups rice and 1 teaspoon salt
- 4 ounces cheddar cheese, vacuum-sealed, home-canned, or waxed

Label each bag

Preheat the oven to 350°F. Start cooking the rice in a small saucepan with 3½ cups of water and the salt. Bring to a boil, cover, reduce the heat, and simmer for 18 minutes. Heat a medium saucepan of water to a simmer, add the broccoli, and cook at a gentle simmer for about 12 minutes until tender. Meanwhile, in a large saucepan over medium heat, melt together the flour and shortening or ghee from the thickener packet, and stir and cook for 3 minutes to make a roux. Open the chicken and drain the liquid into a 4-cup measuring cup or bowl. Stir in the gravy mix and enough water to equal 4 cups. Add the gravy mix liquid to the roux. Over medium-high heat, stir and cook until thickened. Stir in the chicken and vegetables and cook until heated through. Remove from the heat. In a 9 x 13-inch baking dish, layer the rice, broccoli, and chicken mixture. Top with grated cheese and bake 25 to 30 minutes, until bubbly. Let stand for 10 minutes before serving. Serves 8.

Saucy Chicken and Vegetables with Polenta, Mashed Potatoes, Rice, Biscuits, or Naan Ready-Made Meal Assembly (serves 8)

In each of 16 Mylar bags, tote bags, or vacuum bags, store:

- 1 jar or pouch chicken stew mix
- 1 bag thickener
- 1 bag gravy mix
- 1 sidekit Polenta (page 121), Mashed Potatoes (page 122), Rice (page 120), Naan Bread (page 131), or Biscuits (page 126)

Label each bag

Prepare the polenta, mashed potatoes, rice, naan, or biscuits according to the package directions. Meanwhile, in a large saucepan over medium heat, melt together the flour and shortening or ghee from the thickener packet, and stir and cook for 3 minutes to make a roux. Open the chicken and drain the liquid into a 4-cup measuring cup or bowl. Stir in the gravy mix and enough water to equal 4 cups. Add the gravy mix liquid to the roux. Over medium-high heat, stir and cook until thickened. Stir in the chicken and vegetables, and cook until heated through. Serve on top of or alongside the sidekit. Serves 8.

Variation: Turkey and Gravy

All the Classic Chicken and Vegetable recipes above can be made with turkey instead, and they taste like the day after Thanksgiving to me. The nice thing about turkey is that it can be bought very inexpensively around the holidays. Make several of these kits, and enjoy your turkey and your savings throughout the year. In place of the quart-size jars or bags of chicken, store a bag of turkey:

For turkey stew mix: Season the turkey breast with salt and pepper, and cook in a roaster oven at 350°F for about 4 hours or until nearly cooked through. Alternatively, the turkey can be cooked off the bone in a slow cooker set on high or in the oven at 350°F preferably in a covered pot, with about an inch or more of water in the bottom of the roaster/crock/pan. Add more water as needed during the cook time. Meanwhile, mix the soup base or bouillon and water. Adjust the seasoning to taste. When the turkey cook time is up (it needn't be completely done), chop it into bite-size pieces. Add any cooking juices to the soup base or bouillon. Using a canning funnel, fill 16 sterilized quart-size jars or pouches each with 2 cups turkey, 1 cup onions, and ¾ cup each of celery and carrots. Fill with soup base liquid, leaving abundant headspace (1 to 2 inches). Wipe the rims or edges to be sealed, add the lids and rims, or heat-seal the pouches. Pressure-can for 90 minutes.

Chipotle Chicken

This slightly spicy chicken dish is out-of-this-world good, especially served over something to soak up that sauce.

Makes 12 (6 to 8-serving) meals

Ingredients

20 pounds boneless, skinless chicken thighs or breasts, cut into bite-size chunks

olive oil

8 large onions, chopped

3 tablespoons minced garlic

3 (28-ounce) cans diced tomatoes

¼ cup brown sugar, packed

2 (7-ounce) cans chipotle chiles in adobo

salt and pepper

Instructions

Working in batches, pat the chicken chunks dry, season with salt and pepper, and then brown the chicken in 2 tablespoons oil (it needn't be cooked through, just browned). Set aside. Meanwhile, coat a large saucepan with oil and warm over medium-high heat. Cook the onion until it begins to soften. Add the garlic, stir to combine, and then add the tomato sauce and sugar. Puree the chipotles in their sauce in the blender or food processor, and add to the saucepan. Using a canning funnel, fill 12 sterilized quart-size jars or pouches each with 3 cups chicken and then with sauce, leaving abundant headspace (1 to 2 inches). Wipe the rims or edges to be sealed, add the lids and rims, or heat-seal the pouches. Pressure-can for 90 minutes.

 ### Ready-Made Meal Assembly
In each of 12 Mylar bags, tote bags, or vacuum bags, store:

- 1 jar or pouch chipotle chicken
- 1 sidekit Polenta (page 121), Mashed Potatoes (page 122), Buttered Noodles (page 120), Rice (page 120), Naan Bread (page 131), or Biscuits (page 126)

Label each bag
Prepare the polenta, mashed potatoes, buttered noodles, rice, naan, or biscuits according to the package directions. In a large saucepan over medium heat, warm the chipotle chicken until heated through. Serve over or alongside the sidekit. Serves 6 to 8.

Coq Au Vin
(Chicken in Red Wine Sauce)

This is a classic dish that is made even better by pressure canning to allow the flavors to deepen.

Makes 16 (6-serving) meals

Ingredients

24 pounds boneless, skinless chicken thighs or breasts

salt and pepper

olive oil

4 pounds carrots, peeled and cut into 1-inch lengths

4 pounds pearl onions or yellow or white onions, chopped

2 pounds mushrooms, sliced or quartered

5 tablespoons minced garlic

⅔ cup butter

1¼ cups clear jel

3 quarts chicken stock or equivalent soup base and water

3 quarts dry red wine

12 ounces tomato paste

5 tablespoons red currant jelly

5 tablespoons brown sugar, packed

1½ tablespoons dried thyme

5 bay leaves

Instructions

Working in batches, chop the chicken into chunks, season with salt and pepper, and brown the chicken in oil on all sides (it needn't be cooked through, just browned). Coat a large pan with oil and warm over medium-high heat. Cook the carrots, onions, mushrooms, and garlic until they begin to brown. Add the remaining ingredients and stir until well combined. Using a canning funnel, fill 16 sterilized quart-size jars or pouches each with 2½ cups chicken and then with sauce and vegetables, leaving abundant headspace (1 to 2 inches). Wipe the rims or edges to be sealed, add the lids and rims, or heat-seal the pouches. Pressure-can for 90 minutes.

 Ready-Made Meal Assembly

In each of 16 Mylar bags, tote bags, or vacuum bags, store:

- 1 jar or pouch coq au vin

- 1 sidekit Polenta (page 121), Mashed Potatoes (page 122), Buttered Noodles (page 120), Rice (page 120), Naan Bread (page 131), or Biscuits (page 126)

 Label each bag
Prepare the polenta, mashed potatoes, buttered noodles, rice, naan, or biscuits according to the package directions. In a large saucepan over medium heat, warm the coq au vin until heated through. Serve over or alongside the sidekit. Serves 6.

Chicken Piccata

Lemony, bright, and beautiful, chicken piccata is a quintessential chicken dish. I love lemon and caper sauces, so this is a particular favorite of mine.

Makes 16 (4-serving) meals

Ingredients

32 (8-ounce) boneless, skinless chicken breasts

2 cups butter, divided

1 cup olive oil

2 cups flour

2⅔ cups lemon juice

4 cups chicken stock or equivalent soup base or bouillon granules and water

2 cups brined capers, rinsed

2⅔ cups chopped fresh parsley

salt and pepper

Instructions

Pat the chicken dry and season with salt and pepper. Melt 1 cup of the butter with the olive oil in a large skillet over medium-high heat. Working in batches, cook the chicken in half butter and half olive oil, reserving 1 cup of butter to finish the sauce. Brown the chicken breasts on both sides (it doesn't need to be cooked through, just browned), remove from the pan, and set aside. In the same pan, add the remaining ingredients and stir to combine. Cook for 5 minutes. Using a canning funnel, fill 16 sterilized quart-size jars or pouches each with 2 chicken breasts and then with sauce and vegetables, leaving abundant headspace (1 to 2 inches). Wipe the rims or edges to be sealed, add the lids and rims, or heat-seal the pouches. Pressure-can for 90 minutes.

 Ready-Made Meal Assembly

In each of 16 Mylar bags, tote bags, or vacuum bags, store:

- 1 jar or pouch chicken piccata

- 1 sidekit Polenta (page 121), Mashed Potatoes (page 122), Buttered Noodles (page 120), Rice (page 120), Naan Bread (page 131), or Biscuits (page 126)

 Label each bag

Prepare the polenta, mashed potatoes, buttered noodles, rice, naan, or biscuits according to the package directions. In a large skillet over medium heat, warm the chicken piccata until heated through. Serve over or alongside the sidekit. Serves 4.

Turkey Roulade

The tender turkey in this recipe pairs beautifully with the salty prosciutto and tangy feta.

Makes 8 (4-serving) meals

Ingredients

4 boneless whole turkey breasts or 8 half breasts

16 slices prosciutto or other thin ham

1 pound feta cheese, crumbled

¼ cup vegetable oil

½ cup vegetable shortening

salt and pepper

Instructions

Butterfly each turkey breast by cutting it horizontally almost in half and opening it like a book. Place on plastic wrap. Pat the turkey dry and season both sides with salt and pepper. Cut the turkey so it is no more than 8 inches long on the short side. If there is extra, cut it off and layer it atop the turkey at a thin spot. Cover the turkey with a layer of prosciutto or other ham and sprinkle with feta. Using the plastic wrap as an aid, roll up the turkey, beginning with the short side. Tie with kitchen string to secure the roll. Warm the oil in a large skillet over medium-high heat, and brown the turkey. Insert turkey into a canning pouch and make sure it will fit with room to close, leaving abundant headspace (1 to 2 inches). Insert 1 tablespoon shortening. Wipe the edges to be sealed and heat-seal the pouch. Pressure-can for 90 minutes.

 Ready-Made Meal Assembly
In each of 8 Mylar bags, tote bags, or vacuum bags, store:

- 1 pouch turkey

- 1 sidekit Polenta (page 121), Mashed Potatoes (page 122), Buttered Noodles (page 120), or Rice (page 120)

 Label each bag
Prepare the polenta, mashed potatoes, buttered noodles, or rice according to the package directions. In a large skillet over medium heat, brown the turkey, rotating until heated through. Remove the string. Slice and serve over or alongside the sidekit. Serves 4.

Beef Stroganoff

This recipe made with tender beef, mushrooms, and tangy sour cream gravy is practically an American icon. It is really an elegant dish and a family favorite.

Makes 16 (6-serving) meals

Ingredients

24 pounds beef roast, such as chuck

olive oil

8 onions, chopped

5 pounds mushrooms, sliced or quartered

6 quarts beef stock or equivalent soup base and water

1 bottle dry red wine, such as cabernet

8 tablespoons Dijon mustard

5 tablespoons dried thyme

4 cups flour

8 cups sour cream powder

4 cups ghee, canned in 16 (2-ounce) jars

salt and pepper

Instructions

For beef stew: Working in batches, chop the beef into chunks, season with salt and pepper, and brown the beef in oil on all sides (it needn't be cooked through, just browned). When the beef is all cooked, remove it from the pan and set it aside. Add more oil to the pan and cook the onions and mushrooms until they begin to soften. Add the beef stock, wine, Dijon, and thyme, and simmer for about 20 minutes. Using a canning funnel, fill 16 sterilized quart-size jars or pouches each with 2½ cups of beef and then with sauce and vegetables, leaving abundant headspace (1 to 2 inches). Wipe the rims or edges to be sealed, add the lids and rims, or heat-seal the pouches. Pressure-can for 90 minutes.

For flour: In each of 16 zip-top bags, add and then seal:

- ¼ cup flour

For sour cream: In each of 16 zip-top bags, add and then seal:

- ½ cup sour cream powder

Ready-Made Meal Assembly

In each of 16 Mylar bags, tote bags, or vacuum bags, store:

- 1 jar or pouch beef stew
- 1 jar ghee
- 1 packet flour

- 1 packet sour cream powder
- 1 sidekit Mashed Potatoes (page 122), Buttered Noodles (page 120), or Rice (page 120)

Label each bag

Prepare the mashed potatoes, buttered noodles, or rice according to the package directions. In a large saucepan over medium heat, cook the butter and flour together, stirring, about 4 minutes. Add the beef stew and stir well. Heat to simmering, and stir frequently until thickened. Stir in the sour cream packet, adding water if needed for a creamy sauce. Serve over or alongside the sidekit. Serves 6.

Chapter 8

Ready-Made Meals Sidekits

Rice Sidekit

Makes 16 (8-serving) sidekits

Ingredients
20 pounds white rice

¾ cup salt

Instructions
In each of 16 vacuum bags, add and then seal:

- 3 cups white rice
- 2 teaspoons salt

 Label each bag
In a medium saucepan with a lid, combine the rice, salt, and 6 cups of water. Bring to a boil over high heat, cover, and reduce the heat to low. Cook for 18 to 20 minutes. Serves 8.

Buttered Noodles

Makes 16 (8-serving) sidekits

Ingredients
12 pounds pasta

2 cups salt

2 pounds ghee

Instructions
In each of 16 vacuum bags, add and then seal:

- 1 pound pasta or noodles
- 2 tablespoons salt
- 1 (2-ounce) jar ghee or olive oil (optional)

Label each bag
Fill a large pot two-thirds full with water and bring to a boil over high heat. Add the pasta or noodles and salt and cook for 8 to 10 minutes, or until just al dente. Drain and toss with the ghee or olive oil. Serves 8.

Grits

Makes 16 (8-serving) sidekits

Ingredients

8 cups dry milk

5⅓ cups sour cream powder

5 tablespoons salt

32 cups yellow or white corn grits (not instant) or coarse ground cornmeal

4 cups ghee, canned in ¼-cup portions (optional)

8 cups shredded cheddar cheese, vacuum-sealed in ½-cup portions (optional)

Instructions

In each of 16 zip-top bags, add and then seal:

- ½ cup dry milk
- ⅓ cup sour cream powder
- 1 teaspoon salt

In each of 16 vacuum bags, add and then seal:

- 1 zip-top bag of the dry milk mixture
- 2 cups yellow or white corn grits (not instant)
- 1 can ghee, if using
- 1 packet cheese, if using

Label each bag

In a medium saucepan, combine the dry milk bag and 5 cups of water, and stir to combine. Bring to a boil over high heat and stir in the grits. Reduce the heat to a simmer, and cook, stirring periodically, for 15 to 20 minutes, until cooked through. Remove from the heat and stir in the ghee or cheese, if using. Serves 8.

Polenta

Makes 16 (8-serving) sidekits

Ingredients

½ cup salt

48 cups yellow cornmeal

4 cups ghee, canned in ¼-cup portions (optional)

8 cups finely grated Parmesan cheese (like Kraft brand) vacuum-sealed in ½-cup portions (optional)

Instructions

In each of 16 vacuum bags, add and then seal:

- 1½ tablespoons salt
- 3 cups yellow cornmeal

Optional extras:

- ¼ cup ghee
- ½ cup finely grated Parmesan cheese

Label each bag

In a medium saucepan, bring 6 cups of water to a boil. Gradually whisk in the cornmeal and salt. Reduce the heat to a simmer and cook, stirring frequently, for about 15 minutes, until tender. Turn off the heat and stir in the ghee and cheese, if using. Serves 8.

Mashed Potatoes

Makes 16 (8-serving) sidekits

Ingredients

5 cups plus ⅓ cup dry milk

½ cup salt

2 tablespoons plus 2 teaspoons pepper

48 cups potato flakes

Instructions

For potatoes: In each of 16 vacuum bags, add and then seal:

- ⅓ cup dry milk
- 1 teaspoon salt
- ½ teaspoon pepper
- 3 cups potato flakes

For optional extras: Add 1 or more of the following to the bag with the potato flakes:

- ¼ teaspoon garlic powder
- ⅓ cup powdered sour cream
- 1 tablespoon dried chives
- 4 ounces cheddar cheese, canned, waxed, or freeze-dried
- 2 tablespoons bacon bits
- 2 ounces ghee, canned

Label each bag

In a medium saucepan, bring 4½ cups of water to a boil over high heat and remove from the heat. Add the potato flake mixture and stir to combine. Leftovers may be formed into patties and pan-fried until golden for potato pancakes. Serves 8.

Dinner Rolls

Makes 8 (24-roll) sidekits

Ingredients

10 pounds flour

2½ cups sugar

3 tablespoons salt

2 cups dry milk

½ cup active dry yeast

1 cup powdered eggs

4 cups ghee, canned in ¼-pints

Instructions

For flour mixture: In a very large bowl, mix together the flour, sugar, salt, and dry milk.

For yeast: In each of 16 small zip-top bags, add and seal:

- 1 tablespoon yeast

In each of 16 vacuum bags, add and then seal:

- 5½ cups flour mixture
- 2 tablespoons powdered eggs
- 1 packet yeast
- 1 ¼-pint ghee

Label each bag

In a large bowl, mix the yeast with 1½ cups of lukewarm water. Let sit for 5 minutes. Melt the ghee if solid. Measure out ½ cup of the flour mixture and set aside. Add the remainder of the flour mixture and the ghee to the yeast and water and stir well to combine. Add as much of the ½ cup of flour as needed to make a soft but not sticky dough. Knead for 5 minutes. Lightly butter a bowl. Add the dough, and then flip it over. Cover it with a damp towel and put it in a warm place to rise until doubled, about an hour. Grease a 9 x 13-inch baking pan. Divide the dough into 24 balls and place them in the pan, cover with the towel, and let rise again until doubled, about 45 minutes. Preheat the oven to 375°F. Bake for 20 to 25 minutes, until golden brown. Makes 24.

4-Hour Baguettes

Makes 8 sidekits (three 14-inch baguettes each)

Ingredients

3 tablespoons active dry yeast

¼ cup kosher salt

¼ cup vegetable oil

28 cups flour (about 8 pounds)

Instructions

For the yeast: In each of 8 vacuum bags, add and then seal:

- 1 teaspoon yeast

For the salt: In each of 8 vacuum bags, add and then seal:

- ½ tablespoon salt

For the oil: In each of 8 vacuum bags or condiment cups, seal:

- ½ tablespoon vegetable oil

In each of 8 vacuum bags, add and then seal:

- 3½ cups flour
- 1 packet salt
- 1 packet or container oil (optional)

Label each bag

Warm 1½ cups of water to about 115°F, pour into a large wide bowl, and stir in the yeast. Let stand for 10 minutes, until foamy. Set aside ¼ cup of flour and reserve for kneading. Add the remaining flour to the yeast and stir with a fork until a dough forms. Let stand for 20 minutes to allow the flour to absorb the water, and then stir in the salt. Sprinkle the reserved flour on a work surface and knead the dough until smooth, about 10 minutes. Oil a clean bowl and add the dough. Cover with plastic wrap and let sit in a warm place until doubled in size, about 45 minutes. Turn the dough out onto your work surface and press into about an 8 x 6-inch rectangle. Fold the 2 long sides up and over to meet in the middle, and fold the 2 shorter sides up an over to meet in the middle. Return the dough to the bowl, seam-side down, and let rise again until doubled, about 1 hour. Preheat the oven to 475°F. Position a rack in the lowest position of the oven. Place a pan on the rack and pour water into it to create steam while the bread bakes. Place another rack above that and add a baking stone or large baking sheet. Divide the dough into thirds and roll each third into a fat rope about 12 to 14 inches long. Place each rope on parchment paper, leaving enough extra paper at the ends to use for transferring the bread to the oven. Slash each loaf in 4 (4-inch) cuts about ¼-inch deep. Using the parchment paper, transfer the bread to the oven onto the baking stone or baking sheet. Add 4 or 5 ice cubes or ¼ cup water to the lower pan. Bake for about 30 minutes or until deep golden brown. Makes 3 (14-inch) baguettes.

Popovers

Makes 8 sidekits (12 popovers each)

Ingredients

1 ounce ghee or vegetable shortening packaged in 2-tablespoon portions in small plastic containers

2 tablespoons powdered eggs

1 cup flour

⅓ cup dry milk

½ teaspoon salt

Instructions

In each of 16 vacuum bags, add and then seal:

- 1 packet ghee or vegetable shortening
- 2 tablespoons powdered eggs
- 1 cup flour
- ⅓ cup dry milk
- ½ teaspoon salt

Label each bag

Preheat the oven to 450°F. With the shortening or ghee, generously butter 12 cups of a standard muffin tin. Add 1 cup plus 2 tablespoons of water to the popover mix and stir well. Let sit for 10 minutes, then divide the popover mix among the prepared muffin cups and bake for 20 to 25 minutes, until golden and puffed. Makes 12.

Biscuits: Cheddar Garlic Biscuits, Sweet Cinnamon Roll Biscuits

Makes 8 (8-serving) sidekits

Ingredients

23 cups flour (about 5 pounds plus 3 cups)

½ cup baking powder

3 tablespoons salt

1½ tablespoons cream of tartar

1 tablespoon baking soda

3 cups dry milk

6 cups vegetable shortening

Instructions

In a very large bowl, mix together all the dry ingredients except the dry milk. Cut in the shortening with a pastry blender until the mixture resembles coarse crumbs.

In each of 16 vacuum bags, add and then seal:

- 4 cups flour mixture
- ⅓ cup dry milk

Optional—For cheddar garlic biscuits add:

- 4 ounces vacuum-sealed or waxed cheddar cheese
- 2 ounces canned ghee
- ½ teaspoon garlic salt

Optional—For cinnamon rolls add:

- 2 ounces canned ghee
- ½ cup brown sugar vacuum-sealed with ½ teaspoon cinnamon and ½ cup nuts

Label each bag

Preheat the oven to 450°F. Grease a rimmed baking sheet. In a large bowl, combine the flour mixture, dry milk, and 1 cup of water. Stir to combine. Either roll out the dough ½-inch thick and cut with a biscuit cutter, or drop onto the prepared baking sheet by spoonfuls for drop biscuits. Bake for 10 to 12 minutes, until golden brown. Makes about 16 large biscuits.

Optional—For cheddar garlic biscuits: Grate the cheese and add to dough. Bake as usual. Add the garlic salt to the ghee and brush over the tops of the hot biscuits as they come out of the oven.

Optional—For cinnamon rolls: Roll out the dough into a rectangle ½ inch thick. Melt the ghee and pour over the dough, spreading to coat. Sprinkle on the sugar and nut mixture, dispersing it evenly. Roll up from a long side, jelly-roll style. Cut into slices and bake as directed.

Pie Crust

Makes enough for 20 single-crust pies or 10 double-crust pies

Ingredients

5 pounds flour (20 cups)

2 tablespoons salt

3 pounds vegetable shortening (6 cups)

Instructions

Combine the flour and salt in a large bowl. Using a pastry cutter, cut in the shortening until the mixture looks like coarse crumbs.

In 20 vacuum bags, add and then seal:

- 1¼ cups pie crust mix

 Label each bag
Mix the pie crust mix with about 1½ tablespoons of cold water. Roll out between 2 layers of waxed paper. Bake according to the recipe directions.

Cheddar Cheese Pie Crust

Makes 1 crust

Ingredients

1¼ cups pie crust mix (1 Pie Crust Sidekit)

½ cup freeze-dried cheddar cheese

Instructions

For cheese: In a zip-top bag add and then seal

- ½ cup freeze-dried cheddar cheese

In a vacuum a bag, add and then seal:

- 1¼ cups pie crust mix
- 1 bag freeze-dried cheddar cheese

 Label each bag
Soak the cheese in ¼ cup of water for 10 minutes, the drain off the excess water. Mix the pie crust mix with the rehydrated cheese and about 1 tablespoon of cold water. Roll out between 2 layers of waxed paper. Bake according to the recipe directions. Makes 1.

Cornbread, Corn Muffins, or Corn Pancakes

Makes 8 sidekits, which will each make 1 (8 x 8-inch) pan of 2-inch-tall cornbread, or 1 (9 x 13-inch) pan of 1-inch tall cornbread, or about 12 corn muffins

Ingredients

8 cups flour

1½ cups sugar

½ cup baking powder

2 tablespoons salt

2 cups vegetable shortening

9 cups cornmeal

2⅔ cups dry milk

½ cup powdered eggs

Instructions

In a large bowl, mix the flour, sugar, baking powder, and salt. Add shortening and cut in with a pastry cutter until evenly distributed. Add the cornmeal, dry milk, and powdered eggs and mix thoroughly.

In each of 8 vacuum bags, add and then seal:

• 3 cups cornbread mix

Label each bag

For cornbread or muffins: Preheat the oven to 425°F and butter a baking dish or 12 cups of a standard muffin tin. Combine the cornbread mix and 1¼ cups of water. Stir briefly and pour into the prepared baking dish or divide among the muffin cups. Bake an 8 x 8-inch pan of bread for about 25 minutes, a 9 x 13-inch pan for 20 to 25 minutes, and muffins for 15 to 20 minutes. For pancakes, mix as above and cook by ¼ cupfuls on a medium heat skillet in oil for 4 to 5 minutes per side. Makes 1 (8 x 8-inch) pan of 2-inch-tall cornbread, or 1 (9 x 13-inch) pan of 1-inch tall cornbread, or about 12 corn muffins.

Flour Tortillas

Makes 12 sidekits (about 8 tortillas each)

Ingredients

3 cups vegetable shortening

24 cups flour (5 pounds plus 4 cups)

4 tablespoons salt

3 teaspoons baking powder

Instructions

For shortening: Wrap ¼ cup of shortening very well in plastic wrap or place in 4-ounce disposable plastic containers with lids and seal well.

In each of 12 vacuum bags, add and then seal:

- 2 cups flour
- 1 teaspoon salt
- ¼ teaspoon baking powder
- 1 package shortening

Label each bag

Combine all the dry ingredients, then cut in the shortening. Add ⅔ cup of water and mix well into a ball of dough. Divide the dough into 8 pieces. Sprinkle a work surface with flour and roll out each dough piece to ⅛ inch thick. Cook one tortilla at a time in a hot skillet for about 1 minute on each side or until lightly brown in spots. Fill with taco fillings and serve. Makes 8.

Variation: 4-Tortilla Sidekits

To make smaller sidekits perfect for pairing with 4-serving recipes such as Breakfast Burritos (page 37), simply divide the ingredients among 24 vacuum bags, using half the amount of ingredients listed above per bag.

Corn Tortillas

Makes 12 sidekits (about 15 tortillas each)

Ingredients

21 cups masa harina

7 tablespoons salt

Instructions

In each of 12 vacuum bags, add and then seal:

- 1¾ cups masa harina
- 1 teaspoon salt

Label each bag

In a medium bowl, mix together the masa harina and 1⅛ cups of hot water until thoroughly combined. Turn the dough onto a clean work surface and knead until pliable and smooth. If the dough is too sticky, add more masa harina; if it begins to dry out, sprinkle with water. Cover the dough tightly with plastic wrap and allow to stand for 30 minutes.

Preheat a cast-iron skillet or griddle to medium-high. Divide the dough into 15 equal-size balls. Using a tortilla press, a rolling pin, or your hands, press each ball of dough flat between 2 sheets of plastic wrap.

Immediately place a tortilla in the preheated pan and allow to cook for about 30 seconds on one side, or until browned and slightly puffy. Turn the tortilla over to brown on the second side for about 30 seconds more, and then transfer to a plate. Repeat with the remaining balls of dough. Makes about 15.

Naan Bread

Makes 8 sidekits (6 to 8 pieces each)

Ingredients

8 (2¼-teaspoon) packages store-bought active dry yeast or 8 packets vacuum-sealed each containing ½ tablespoon

1 pound ghee

36 cups flour

2 cups sugar

½ cup dry milk

½ cup powdered eggs

3½ tablespoons salt

Instructions

For yeast (if not using store-bought): In each of 8 small vacuum bags or zip-top bags, add and then seal:

- ½ tablespoon yeast

For ghee: In each of 8 small jars or disposable containers with lids, seal:

- ¼ cup (2 ounces) ghee

In each of 8 vacuum bags, add and then seal:

- 1 packet yeast
- 4½ cups flour
- ¼ cup sugar
- 1 tablespoon dry milk
- 1 tablespoon powdered eggs
- 2 teaspoons salt
- 1 jar ghee

Label each bag

In a large bowl, dissolve the yeast in 1¼ cups of warm water. Let stand for about 10 minutes, until frothy. Stir in the flour, sugar, dry milk, and powdered eggs to make a soft dough. On a lightly floured surface, knead for 6 to 8 minutes, or until smooth. Place the dough in an oiled bowl, cover with a damp cloth, and set aside for 1 hour, or until doubled in volume.

Punch down the dough, knead lightly, and pinch off small handfuls of dough about the size of golf balls. Roll into balls, cover with the towel, and let rest, for about 30 minutes.

Meanwhile, preheat a grill, grill pan, or griddle on high heat until hot.

One at a time, roll dough balls into flat circles, lightly oil the pan or grill, and cook for 2 to 3 minutes, or until puffy and lightly browned. Brush the uncooked sides with the ghee, and turn over. Brush the cooked sides with ghee, and cook until the second sides are browned, another 2 to 4 minutes. Remove from the grill, and repeat with the remaining dough.

Syrup Sidekit

A great alternative to maple syrup, this syrup "kit" is less expensive, can be packed dry, and everyone loves it.

Makes 16 (⅔-cup) bags

Ingredients

10⅔ cups brown sugar

2 teaspoons salt

Instructions

In each of 16 vacuum bags, add and then seal:

- ⅔ cup brown sugar
- pinch of salt

Label each bag
To prepare 1 serving, in a small pot, combine packet and ⅓ cup of water, and stir over low heat until sugar is dissolved.

Vegetable Sidekits

Asparagus

Asparagus can be dehydrated or canned. To dehydrate, wash and cut into 1-inch pieces. Dehydrate at 120°F for 5 to 6 hours. To pressure-can asparagus, fill pint- or quart-size jars or retort pouches with asparagus, cover with boiling water, and seal well. Follow USDA pressure-canning guidelines and process 30 minutes for pints and 40 minutes for quarts.

Beans, dry

It is super-convenient and economical to have cooked beans on hand. Cover beans in 2 to 3 times their volume of water and soak for 12 to 18 hours. Drain. In a large pot, cover again with about 3 times the volume of water, salt abundantly (about 2 tablespoons salt per gallon of water), and bring to a boil over high heat. Reduce the heat to low and simmer gently for 30 minutes. Pack in sterilized jars or retort pouches, leaving 1 to 2 inches headspace, with the cooking water up to the level of the beans. Seal well. Follow USDA pressure-canning guidelines and process 75 minutes for pints and 90 minutes for quarts.

1 pound dried beans is the same as about 2 cups, which will yield 4 to 5 cups of cooked beans. When canned, the yield is about 2½ pints or 1¼ quarts.

Baked Beans

Combine 1 quart beans canned as above with ½ cup barbecue sauce. Heat gently until heated through and serve.

Beets

Beets need to be boiled, peeled, and possibly chopped depending on size before they are canned or dehydrated. Boil beets in a pot with plenty of water, 15 minutes for small beets, 20 minutes for large beets. Remove from the water and peel when cool enough to handle. Baby beets may be left whole, but larger beets should be chopped and either dehydrated at 120°F for 8 to 12 hours or canned. For canned beets, ladled into sterile pint- or quart-size canning jars or retort pouches and fill with water. Leave 1 to 2 inches headspace and seal well. Follow USDA pressure-canning guidelines and process 30 minutes for pints and 35 minutes for quarts. Beets are also delicious with a pinch of powdered vanilla added before canning.

Beet Soup

Add 2 teaspoons chicken or vegetable soup base and ½ teaspoon each garlic and onion powder and process through a food mill. Package along with ½ cup of sour cream powder, which you mix with ¼ cup of water to make a sour cream soup topping.

Broccoli

Broccoli can be blanched and then dehydrated at about 120°F for 12 to 14 hours. It is not recommended to can broccoli, because the florets become pulverized in the processing and the smell of the broccoli is greatly concentrated to an unappealing degree. Mushy and smelly.

Carrots

Carrots can be either dehydrated or canned. Peel them first. Then, to dehydrate, slice thinly and dehydrate at 120°F for 6 to 10 hours. To can, leave whole or chop. Fill into quart- or pint-size jars or retort pouches and cover with boiling water. Leave 1 to 2 inches headspace and seal well. Follow USDA pressure-canning guidelines and process 25 minutes for pints and 30 minutes for quarts.

Carrot Soup

Add 2 teaspoons chicken or vegetable soup base and 1 teaspoon ground ginger to each quart of carrots and can as above. When you open the jar or pouch, strain the water into a soup pot and process the carrots through a food mill. Stir well and heat until simmering. Serve with Cornbread (page 128).

Glazed Carrots

In a zip-top bag, package together 2 tablespoons butter-flavored vegetable shortening wrapped well in plastic or 2 tablespoons canned ghee and 3 tablespoons brown sugar. Seal together with a quart of carrots in a Mylar bag. To serve, drain off the carrot liquid (save for another purpose) and reheat the carrots gently in melted shortening or ghee and stir in the brown sugar. Serve when heated through, about 5 minutes.

Chimichurri Carrots

Package Chimichurri mix (page 149) with the carrots. Prepare the chimichurri according to the package directions. Drain the carrots into a saucepan. Add the chimichurri and stir to combine. Warm gently and serve.

Green Beans

Green beans can be dehydrated or canned. To dehydrate, wash the beans, clean the ends, and cut into 1-inch pieces. Dehydrate at 120°F for 8 to 12 hours. To can green beans, fill quart- or pint-size jars or retort pouches and cover with boiling water, leaving 1 to 2 inches headspace. Seal well. Follow USDA pressure-canning guidelines and process 20 minutes for pints and 25 minutes for quarts.

Green Beans with Bacon

Cut bacon into lardons (crosswise into ½-inch strips), pan-fry until very crispy, and then dehydrate at 120°F for 6 to 8 hours, turning and blotting up excess oil twice during the drying time. Vacuum-seal into ¼-cup servings (for quarts) or 2 tablespoons (for pints) and package with green beans to sprinkle on top before serving.

Green Beans and Almonds

Vacuum-seal ¼-cup packets (for quarts) or 2 tablespoons (for pints) of sliced almonds and package with green beans. Toast briefly in a small pan before serving sprinkled over the beans.

Lemon Pepper Beans

Package 4 slices of dehydrated lemon and 1 teaspoon lemon pepper (for quarts) or ½ teaspoon (for pints) and package with green beans. To serve, reheat the beans in their liquid, then add the lemon slices. Heat gently for 10 minutes, then drain off the excess water, sprinkle with lemon pepper, and serve.

Greens

Greens can be dehydrated or canned. To dehydrate, wash the greens, remove any tough stems, and tear into 1-inch pieces. Dehydrate at 120°F for 6 to 8 hours. To can greens, boil or steam them first for about 4 minutes. Fill quart- or pint-size jars or retort pouches with greens and cover with boiling water, leaving 1 to 2 inches headspace. Seal well. Follow USDA pressure-canning guidelines and process 70 minutes for pints and 90 minutes for quarts.

Garlicky Greens

Package together 1 tablespoon vegetable shortening and 1 teaspoon garlic powder for each quart of greens (½ tablespoon and ½ teaspoon, respectively, for pints) and package with the greens. To serve, melt the shortening in a pot and drain off most of the water from the greens. Add the greens and garlic powder to the shortening and stir gently until heated through.

Spicy Greens

Package together 1 tablespoon butter-flavored vegetable shortening and 1 teaspoon red pepper flakes for each quart of greens (½ tablespoon and ½ teaspoon, respectively, for pints) and package with the greens. To serve, melt the shortening in a pot and drain off most of the water from the greens. Add the greens and red pepper flakes to the shortening and stir gently until heated through.

Corn

Corn can be dehydrated or canned. To dehydrate, cut the kernels from the cobs, spread on trays, and dehydrate at 120°F for 12 to 24 hours until completely dry. To can, fill into quart- or pint-size jars or retort pouches and cover with boiling water, leaving 1 to 2 inches headspace. Seal well. Follow USDA pressure-canning guidelines and process 55 minutes for pints and 80 minutes for quarts.

Buttered and Salty Corn

Package 1 tablespoon butter-flavored vegetable shortening or ghee and 1 teaspoon salt for each quart of corn (½ tablespoon and ½ teaspoon, respectively, for pints). Melt the shortening or ghee in a pot and then add corn and reheat gently.

Southwest Corn

Package 1 teaspoon salt and 3 tablespoons dehydrated red or green bell peppers for each quart of corn (½ teaspoon salt and 1½ tablespoons peppers for pints). Add the corn and their liquid to a pot, add the peppers and salt, and heat gently for at least 10 minutes to allow the peppers to rehydrate.

Peas

Peas can be dehydrated or canned. To dehydrate peas, steam them first until just tender, and then dehydrate at 120°F for 8 to 12 hours. To can peas, fill raw into quart- or pint-size jars or retort pouches and cover with boiling water, leaving 1 to 2 inches headspace. Seal well. Follow USDA pressure-canning guidelines and process 40 minutes for both pints and quarts.

Lemon Butter Peas

Package 1 tablespoon butter-flavored vegetable shortening or ghee and 4 slices dehydrated lemon for each quart of peas (½ tablespoon and 2 slices, respectively, for pints). Melt the shortening in a pot with the lemon and then add peas and reheat gently.

Peppers

Peppers are best roasted and peeled before canning or dehydrating. Sear the peppers under a broiler or on a stove burner until black and blistered on all sides. Place in a bowl and cover with plastic wrap. Let steam and then peel off the skins, core, and chop. Dehydrate at 120°F for 12 to 24 hours or fill into quart- or pint-size jars or retort pouches and cover with boiling water, leaving 1 to 2 inches headspace. Seal well. Follow USDA pressure-canning guidelines and process 35 minutes for pints. It is not recommended to can quarts of peppers.

Potatoes

To dehydrate or can potatoes, add 1 teaspoon ascorbic acid (vitamin C) to a quart of water in a pot to keep the potatoes from turning dark. For dehydrating, steam or boil the potatoes in plain water until just barely tender and then dice, dip into the water bath with the ascorbic acid, and dehydrate at 120°F for about 12 hours. To can, peel and dice the potatoes raw and dip in the water bath. Fill into quart- or pint-size jars or retort pouches and cover with boiling water, leaving 1 to 2 inches headspace. Seal well. Follow USDA pressure-canning guidelines and process 35 minutes for pints and 40 minutes for quarts.

Pumpkin or Other Winter Squash

For dehydrating, peel the pumpkins or squash, steam or boil until just barely tender, and then dice and dehydrate at 120°F for 12 to 15 hours. To can, peel, dice, and steam for 15 minutes. Fill into quart- or pint-size jars or retort pouches and cover with boiling water, leaving 1 to 2 inches headspace. Seal well. Follow USDA pressure-canning guidelines and process 55 minutes for pints and 90 minutes for quarts.

Pumpkin or Winter Squash Soup

Vacuum-seal together 1 teaspoon salt, ½ teaspoon pepper, and ¼ teaspoon each ground ginger, cayenne pepper, and allspice. Separately vacuum-seal ¼ cup of pumpkin seeds (pepitas). If using dehydrated squash, cover in hot water and soak for 10 minutes. Process the canned squash or rehydrated dried squash through a food mill into a soup pot, add the spices and liquid from the can (or soaking liquid), and stir. Heat gently to a simmer and serve topped with pumpkin seeds.

Sweet Potatoes

For dehydrating, peel the sweet potatoes, steam or boil until just barely tender, and then dice and dehydrate at 120°F for 12 to 15 hours. To can, peel, dice, and steam for 15 minutes. Fill into quart- or pint-size jars or retort pouches and cover with boiling water, leaving 1 to 2 inches headspace. Seal well. Follow USDA pressure-canning guidelines and process 65 minutes for pints and 90 minutes for quarts.

Sweet Potato Casserole

Separately vacuum-seal 2 tablespoons butter-flavored vegetable shortening or ghee, 2 cups mini marshmallows, 2 teaspoons salt, and 1 teaspoon ground cinnamon. To prepare the casserole, preheat the oven to 350°F. Soak dehydrated potatoes in hot water for 10 minutes to rehydrate. Drain the sweet potatoes, mash, and mix with the melted shortening or ghee and cinnamon. Put in a baking dish, top with the marshmallows, and bake for 30 minutes.

Fruited Rice Pilaf Mix

Makes 12 (8-serving) sidekits

Ingredients

16 cups uncooked long-grain white rice

4 cups golden raisins

3 cups chopped dried apricots

¾ cup dehydrated minced onion

¾ cup chicken soup base or bouillon granules

¼ cup sugar

1 tablespoon pepper

Instructions

Stir together all the ingredients in a large bowl.

In each of 12 vacuum bags, add and then seal:

- 1¾ cups rice mix

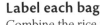
Label each bag
Combine the rice mix and 2 cups of water in a medium saucepan with a lid. Bring to a boil over high heat. Reduce the heat to a simmer, cover, and cook for 18 to 20 minutes, until the water is absorbed and the rice is tender. Serves 8.

Chicken Roni Pasta Rice

Makes 12 (8-serving) sidekits

Ingredients

12 cups long-grain white rice

6 cups small pasta, like orzo, or spaghetti, broken into ½-inch pieces

1 cup chicken soup base or bouillon granules

¼ cup dried parsley flakes

2 tablespoons garlic powder

1½ cups butter-flavored vegetable shortening

Instructions

For rice packet: In each of 12 vacuum bags, add and then seal:

- 1 cup long-grain white rice
- ½ cup pasta

For seasoning pouch: In each of 12 vacuum bags, add and then seal:

- 1½ tablespoons chicken soup base or bouillon granules
- 1 teaspoon dried parsley flakes
- ½ teaspoon garlic powder

For shortening: Wrap 12 (2-tablespoon) portions of shortening in plastic wrap.

 Ready-Made Meal Assembly
In each of 12 vacuum bags, add and then seal:

- 1 rice packet
- 1 seasoning pouch
- 1 packet shortening

 Label each bag
To prepare, in a large skillet with a lid, melt the shortening over medium-high heat, then brown the pasta and rice until the pasta is light golden brown. Add 2 cups of water, bring to a boil, and add the seasoning packet. Stir to combine. Reduce the heat to low, cover, and simmer for about 20 minutes, until the water is absorbed and the rice is tender. Serves 8.

Curried Rice Mix

Makes 12 (8-serving) bags

Ingredients

2 cups dehydrated minced onion

¾ cup curry powder

¾ cup chicken soup base or bouillon granules

4 teaspoons garlic powder

2 teaspoons ground turmeric

24 cups white rice

Instructions

For seasoning: In a medium bowl, mix together all the ingredients except the rice.

In each of 12 vacuum bags, add and then seal:

- 2 cups white rice
- ¼ cup seasoning

Note: You may substitute brown rice for the white rice. Increase the water to 5 cups and increase the cook time to 50 minutes. This rice is also delicious with the addition of raisins and/or chopped almonds.

Label each bag
Combine the rice mix and 4 cups of water in a medium saucepan with lid. Bring to a boil over high heat. Reduce the heat to a simmer, cover, and cook for 18 to 20 minutes, until the water is absorbed and the rice is tender. Serves 12.

Beefy Rice and Mushroom Mix

Makes 12 (8-serving) sidekits

Ingredients

2 cups dehydrated minced onion

¾ cup beef soup base or bouillon granules

2 cups dried parsley flakes

6 cups dried mushrooms

24 cups white rice

Instructions

For seasoning: In a large bowl, mix together all the ingredients except the rice and dried mushrooms.

In each of 12 vacuum bags, add and then seal:

- ½ cup dried mushrooms
- 2 cups white rice

Note: You may substitute brown rice for the white rice. Increase the water to 5 cups and increase the cook time to 50 minutes.

Label each bag
Combine the rice mix and 4 cups of water in a medium saucepan with a lid. Bring to a boil over high heat. Reduce the heat to a simmer, cover, and cook for 18 to 20 minutes, until the water is absorbed and the rice is tender. Serves 8.

Indian Rice with Cashews and Raisins

Makes 8 (8-serving) sidekits

Ingredients

½ cup coconut oil

16 cups basmati rice

3½ tablespoons chicken soup base or bouillon granules

1½ teaspoons ground cumin

1½ teaspoons ground coriander

1 teaspoon red pepper flakes

2 tablespoons plus 2 teaspoons salt

2 teaspoons ground turmeric

6 cups cashews

4 cups seedless golden raisins

8 (13.5-ounce) cans coconut milk

Instructions

For coconut oil: Package 1 tablespoon in each of 8 pieces of plastic wrap and seal well.

For rice mix: In each of 8 vacuum bags, add and then seal:

- 2 cups basmati rice
- 1 teaspoon chicken soup base or bouillon granules
- ½ teaspoon ground cumin
- ½ teaspoon ground coriander
- 1 pinch red pepper flakes
- 1 teaspoon salt
- ¼ teaspoon ground turmeric
- ¾ cup cashews
- ½ cup golden raisins
- 1 packet coconut oil
- 1 (13.5-ounce) can coconut milk

Label each bag
Heat the oil in a large pot over medium-high heat. Stir in the rice mix and cook for 2 minutes. Add the coconut milk and 2½ cups of water. Bring to a boil, then cover and reduce the heat to low. Cook until the rice is tender, about 20 minutes. Serves 8.

Chickeny Rice with Almonds and Dried Cranberries aka "Northwest Pilaf"

This regional combination is delicious. It is my family's favorite.

Makes 12 (8-serving) bags

Ingredients

2 cups dehydrated minced onion

1 cup chicken soup base or bouillon granules

2 cups dried parsley flakes

3 cups sliced almonds

3 cups dried cranberries

24 cups uncooked white rice

Instructions

For seasoning: In a medium bowl, mix together the onion, bouillon, and dried parsley flakes.

For almonds: In each of 12 vacuum bags, add and then seal:

- ½ cup sliced almonds

For dried cranberries: In each of 12 vacuum bags, add and then seal:

- ½ cup dried cranberries

For seasoning mix: In a large bowl, mix together the soup base or bouillon granules and the dried parsley flakes. In each of 12 vacuum bags, add and then seal:

- ¼ cup seasoning mix

For rice mix: In each of 12 vacuum bags, add and then seal:

- 2 cups uncooked white rice
- 1 packet seasoning
- 1 bag almonds
- 1 bag dried cranberries

Note: You may substitute brown rice for the white rice. Increase the water to 5 cups and increase the cook time to 50 minutes.

 **Label each bag**
Combine the rice mix and 4 cups of water in a medium saucepan with a lid. Bring to a boil over high heat. Reduce the heat to a simmer, cover, and cook for 18 to 20 minutes, until the water is absorbed and the rice is tender. Stir in the almonds and dried cranberries and let sit for 5 minutes before serving. Serves 8.

Chapter 9

Snacks, Beverages, and Extras

Popcorn

Makes 8 (16-cup) batches

Ingredients

2 tablespoons plus 2 teaspoons salt

1 cup coconut oil

4 cups popcorn kernels

Instructions

For salt: In each of 8 zip-top bags, add and then seal:

- 1 teaspoon salt

 ### Ready-Made Meal Assembly
In each of 8 vacuum bags, add and then seal:

- 1 packet salt
- 2 tablespoons coconut oil
- ½ cup popcorn kernels

Variations

Add 1 teaspoon lemon pepper or 2 tablespoons finely grated Parmesan cheese (like Kraft brand) to the salt when you package it.

 ### Label each bag
Add all the ingredients to a very large pot with a lid. Heat over high heat, covered, shaking occasionally until the first kernels pop, and then shake more often. Remove from the heat when the popping slows. Makes 16 cups.

Kettle Corn

Makes 8 (16-cup) batches

Ingredients

2 cups sugar

2 tablespoons salt

1 cup coconut oil

4 cups popcorn kernels

Instructions

For coconut oil: Wrap 8 (2-tablespoon) portions of oil in plastic wrap.

For sugar and salt: In each of 8 zip-top bags, add and then seal:

- ¼ cup sugar
- ¼ teaspoon salt

Ready-Made Meal Assembly
In each of 8 vacuum bags, add and then seal:

- 2 packets coconut oil
- ½ cup popcorn kernels
- 1 packet sugar and salt

Label each bag
Add the popcorn and coconut oil to a very large pot with a lid. Heat over high heat, covered, shaking occasionally until the first kernels pop, and then shake more often. When the popping slows, remove from the heat. When the popping stops, add the sugar and salt bag contents and stir very well to distribute seasonings. Serve hot. Makes 16 cups.

Apples

Apples can be canned or dehydrated. Dehydrate sliced apples until completely dry and crisp, about 24 hours at 120°F. Vacuum-seal in 1-cup bags for snacks.

To can sliced apples, first cook in water for 5 minutes with ¼ teaspoon ascorbic acid (vitamin C) to prevent browning and an appropriate amount of sugar depending on the tartness of the apples. For these sliced apples in syrup, follow USDA pressure-canning guidelines and process for 8 minutes. Alternatively, you can cook the apples until they become completely softened into applesauce and then can the applesauce. For applesauce, refer to USDA pressure-canning guidelines and process 15 minutes for pints or 20 minutes for quarts.

Apple Cobbler
Package together 1 quart of apples or applesauce with Cobbler Mix (page 154).

Apple Pie
Package 1 quart of canned apple slices or 4 cups of dried apples with separately packaged 2 Pie Crust Sidekits (page 127), 2 teaspoons ground cinnamon, and 2 tablespoons butter-flavored vegetable shortening or ghee.

 Label each bag
Preheat the oven to 400°F. Roll out the bottom pie crust and place in an 8-inch pie dish. Fill with the apples, sprinkle with cinnamon, and dot with shortening or ghee. Roll out the top pie crust and cover the top of the pie. Crimp and decorate the edges, slit the top decoratively to vent, and bake for about 50 minutes or until golden. Makes 1 (8-inch) pie.

Fruit Roll-Ups

To make fruit roll-ups, cook peeled, pitted, chopped fruit with a small amount of water until soft, about 15 minutes. Taste and add sugar and/or a small amount of lemon as needed. Process the fruit through a food mill. Line a rimmed baking sheet or dehydrator tray with plastic wrap. Pour the fruit on the plastic on the tray to a depth of ⅛ inch. Place in the oven on its "keep-warm" setting or 140°F, or in a dehydrator set for 120°F until dry and leathery. Roll up cigar style in plastic wrap and seal several together in vacuum bags.

Beef Jerky

Bottom round beef is best for this, but you can use anything that's on sale. Ask the meat counter to cut it thinly for you.

Makes about 2 pounds

Ingredients

½ cup soy sauce

½ cup Worcestershire sauce

6 pounds beef, such as bottom round, sliced ¼-inch thick

2 tablespoons black pepper

Instructions

Combine the soy sauce and Worcestershire sauce and marinate the meat in this mixture for about 12 hours. Lay the meat out on trays and sprinkle with pepper. Set the oven to the lowest setting ("keep warm," about 140°F) or a dehydrator to 145°F, and dehydrate the meat for 8 to 12 hours, until completely dry. Vacuum-seal.

Sweet and Savory Spiced Nuts

Makes 6 (4-cup) batches

Ingredients

24 cups unsalted mixed nuts, such as walnuts, pecans, hazelnuts, and almonds

12 ounces ghee or 4 cups butter-flavored vegetable shortening

2 tablespoons ground cumin

2 teaspoons cayenne pepper

2 teaspoons ground cinnamon

2½ cups brown sugar, packed

2 tablespoons salt

Instructions

In each of 8 vacuum bags, add and then seal:

- ¼ cup ghee or ⅔ cup shortening
- 4 cups unsalted mixed nuts
- 2 teaspoons ground cumin
- ½ teaspoon cayenne pepper
- ½ teaspoon ground cinnamon
- 6 tablespoons brown sugar, packed
- 1 teaspoon salt

For the ghee or shortening: in each of 8 vacuum bags, add and then vacuum seal:

- ½ tablespoon ghee or ¾ tablespoon shortening

Label each bag
Heat the nuts in a dry skillet and cook, stirring frequently, until they begin to toast, about 4 minutes. Add the shortening or ghee and cook, stirring, until the nuts begin to darken, about 1 minute. Add the spices and sugar and 1 tablespoon of water, and cook, stirring, until the sauce thickens and the nuts are glazed, about 5 minutes. Makes 4 cups.

Spicy Roasted Chickpeas

Makes 8 (2-cup) batches

Ingredients

5 tablespoons cayenne pepper

5 tablespoons ground cumin

10 tablespoons salt

2 cups vegetable shortening

12 cups dried chickpeas or 16 (14.5-ounce) store-bought cans chickpeas

Instructions

For seasoning: In each of 8 zip-top bags, add and then seal:

- 1 teaspoon cayenne pepper
- 1 teaspoon ground cumin
- 2 teaspoons salt

For shortening: In each of 8 pieces of plastic wrap or 8 disposable containers with lids, add and then seal well:

- ¼ cup of shortening

For dried chickpeas (if using): In each of 8 vacuum bags, seal:

- 1½ cups chickpeas

Ready-Made Meal Assembly
In each of 8 Mylar bags or tote bags, store:

- 1 bag dried chickpeas or 2 store-bought cans chickpeas
- 1 packet seasoning
- 1 packet shortening

Label each bag
For dried chickpeas, soak the chickpeas overnight in enough water to cover by several inches. Drain and replace the water. Boil for 1 hour, drain, cool, and pat dry. For both dried chickpeas and canned chickpeas, preheat the oven to 450°F and melt the shortening. Add the chickpeas and seasonings and stir to coat evenly. Spread on a rimmed baking sheet and roast for 10 to 15 minutes or until crisp and nutty. Makes 2 cups.

Dry Chimichurri

Chimichurri is a fabulous spicy condiment that perks up the flavor of everything. Try it paired with vegetables or eggs. It is especially lovely with carrots.

Makes 8 (¼-cup) batches

Ingredients

½ cup dried parsley

½ cup dehydrated onion flakes

2½ tablespoons dried oregano

2½ tablespoons dehydrated minced garlic

2½ tablespoons red pepper flakes

2½ tablespoons dried basil

2½ tablespoons paprika

1 tablespoon finely crushed bay leaf

2½ tablespoons salt

½ cup water

½ cup apple cider vinegar

1 cup olive oil, vegetable oil, or ghee

Instructions

For dry mix: In a medium bowl, mix together the dried parsley, onion flakes, oregano, minced garlic, red pepper flakes, basil, paprika, bay leaf, and salt.

For water and vinegar: In each of 8 small vacuum bags, add and then seal:

- 1 tablespoon each of water
- 1 tablespoon vinegar

For oil: In each of 8 small vacuum bags, add and then seal:

- 2 tablespoons olive oil, vegetable oil, or ghee

In each of 8 small vacuum bags, add and then seal:

- ¼ cup dry mix
- 1 packet oil
- 1 packet vinegar and water

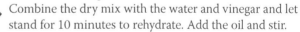

Label each bag
Combine the dry mix with the water and vinegar and let stand for 10 minutes to rehydrate. Add the oil and stir. Drizzle on meats, vegetables, or tacos. Makes ¼ cup.

Beverage Ideas

If you are making tubs to contain a week's worth of meals and snacks, you might like to include some drink mixes too. Some ideas to include:

Instant coffee—Starbucks Via is the best.

Chai tea—Big Train Chai Tea is a delicious, just-add-water drink.

Hot cocoa—A favorite on a cold day.

Tang—Hey, if astronauts drink it …

Kool-Aid—If you are creating weekly or daily meal kits, consider adding packets of Kool-Aid with the measured amount of sugar. It will be all set to mix with water, stir, and serve.

Lemonade—See my recipe below.

Gatorade instant drink mix—Especially helpful for rehydration.

Tea—See page 151 for how to package teabags, lemon, and sugar.

Lemonade

This recipe can also easily be made into limeade or orangeade by changing up the citrus.

Makes 10 kits

Ingredients

20 cups sugar

20 lemons, sliced thin and dehydrated

Instructions

In each of 10 vacuum bags, add and then seal:

- 1 cup sugar
- 2 lemons, sliced (about 20 slices)

Label each bag

Add the sugar and lemons to a large pitcher and fill with water and ice. Stir well to dissolve the sugar. Refrigerate for 1 hour and serve garnished with a lemon slice. Makes 1 pitcher.

Hot Cocoa

Makes 8 (8-serving) batches

Ingredients

16 cups powdered sugar

8 cups cocoa (Dutch-process preferred)

20 cups dry milk

2½ tablespoons salt

2½ tablespoons cornstarch

¼ teaspoon cayenne pepper (optional)

8 cups mini marshmallows (optional)

Instructions

For cocoa mix: In a very large bowl, mix together all the ingredients except the marshmallows.

For marshmallows (if using): In each of 8 zip-top bags, seal:

- 1 cup marshmallows

In each of 8 vacuum bags, add and then seal:

- 4¼ cups cocoa mix
- 1 packet marshmallows (if using)

Label each bag

Fill each serving cup halfway with cocoa mix and then fill the cup with hot water. Stir, top with marshmallows, if using, and enjoy. Makes 8 cups.

Tang

Although it's not a recipe, here are instructions for packaging servings of Tang for 8 people:

Vacuum-seal ⅔ cup of Tang drink mix. Label each bag: "Combine the drink mix with 8 cups (2 quarts) of water in a pitcher and stir."

One 72-ounce canister of Tang will make 22 quarts or 11 packets of Tang for 8.

Tea Kits

In vacuum bags, vacuum-seal together 4 small or 3 large teabags, 8 dehydrated lemon slices, and 16 sugar cubes, or 4 tablespoons sugar and $\frac{1}{3}$ cup of dry milk if you take milk in your tea. For a special treat, add ¼ teaspoon powdered vanilla to the sugar.

Chapter 10
Desserts

Cobbler Mix

Package cobbler mix together with apples, peaches, plums, or any other canned or dried fruit.

Makes 6 (8-serving) bags

Ingredients

6 cups sugar

6 cups flour

1 tablespoon salt

6 tablespoons powdered eggs

1½ teaspoons powdered vanilla

2¼ cups butter-flavored vegetable shortening or ghee

Instructions

For cobbler mix: In each of 6 vacuum bags, Mylar bags, or jars, add and then seal:

- 1 cup sugar
- 1 cup flour
- ½ teaspoon salt
- 1 tablespoon powdered eggs
- ¼ teaspoon powdered vanilla

For shortening or ghee: In each of 6 vacuum bags or jars, add and then seal:

- 6 tablespoons (¼ cup plus 2 tablespoons) shortening or ghee

 Ready-Made Meal Assembly

In a Mylar bag, tote bag, or vacuum bag, store:

- 1 jar or pouch cobbler mix
- 1 packet shortening or ghee

Pair with: 1 quart home-canned fruit or 3 cups dried fruit

 Label each bag

Preheat the oven to 375°F. If using dried fruit, cover in hot water and soak for 10 minutes, then drain off excess water. Spread the fruit evenly in a 10 x 6-inch baking dish. In a large bowl, combine the cobbler mix and 1 to 2 tablespoons of water and mix until crumbly. Sprinkle over the fruit. Melt the shortening or ghee and drizzle over the fruit and topping. Bake for 30 to 35 minutes, until golden brown and bubbly. Serves 8.

Rustic Pie

Package pie crust mix together with apples, peaches, plums, or any other canned or dried fruit.

Makes 12 (8-serving) bags

Ingredients

12½ cups flour

2 tablespoons salt

6 tablespoons egg powder

5 cups vegetable shortening

Instructions

In a large bowl, combine the flour, salt, and egg powder. Mix well. Cut in the shortening until mixture is like coarse crumbs.

In each of 12 vacuum bags, Mylar bags, or jars, add and then seal:

- 1¼ cups pie crust mix

Ready-Made Meal Assembly

In a vacuum or Mylar bag or tote bag, package:

- 1 packet pie crust mix

Pair with: 1 quart home-canned fruit or 3 cups dried fruit

Label

Preheat the oven to 375°F. If using dried fruit, cover in hot water and soak for 10 minutes, then drain off excess water. Combine the pie crust mix with 2 tablespoons of very cold water. Stir to combine. Roll out between sheets of waxed paper. Place on a baking sheet. Mound the fruit in the center of the dough, leaving a 3-inch border. Fold up edges over the fruit and bake for about 50 minutes, until flaky and golden. Cool before serving. Serves 8.

No-Bake Cookies

I love these cookies. The shelf life of peanut butter is about two years, but I am sure you'll get through these kits faster than that!

Makes 6 batches (about 3 dozen cookies each)

Ingredients

3 cups butter-flavored vegetable shortening or ghee in ½-cup packages

12 cups sugar

1½ cups dry milk

1½ teaspoons powdered vanilla

2 cups cocoa powder

18 cups instant oats

3 cups dry roasted peanuts (optional)

3 cups peanut butter, creamy or chunky

Instructions

For shortening or ghee: In each of 6 vacuum bags or jars, seal:

- ½ cup of ghee or shortening

For sugar and milk: In each of 6 vacuum bags, add and then seal:

- 3 cups sugar
- ¼ cup dry milk
- ¼ teaspoon powdered vanilla

For oats and cocoa: In each of 6 vacuum bags or zip-top bags, add and then seal:

- ⅓ cup cocoa powder
- 3 cups instant oats
- ½ cup dry roasted peanuts

For peanut butter: In each of 6 vacuum bags or disposable 4-ounce containers, add and then seal:

- ½ cup (4 ounces) peanut butter, creamy or chunky

Ready-Made Meal Assembly

In each of 6 Mylar bags, tote bags, or vacuum bags, store:

- 1 bag or jar shortening or ghee
- 1 bag sugar and milk
- 1 bag oats and cocoa
- 1 bag or container peanut butter

Label each bag

In a large saucepan, heat the shortening or ghee until melted. Add the sugar and milk packet and ½ cup of water and stir to combine. Heat until boiling and boil for 1 minute, timing it carefully. Add the peanut butter and stir to melt. Add the oats, cocoa, and peanut packet and stir to combine. Drop by heaping spoonfuls onto waxed paper. Cool and serve. Makes about 3 dozen.

Oatmeal Cookies with M&Ms

Makes 6 batches (4 dozen cookies each)

Ingredients

16½ cups rolled oats

4½ cups sugar

4½ cups flour

4½ cups M&Ms

4½ teaspoons salt

4 teaspoons baking soda

6 tablespoons dry milk

6 tablespoons powdered eggs

1 tablespoon powdered vanilla

4½ cups of butter-flavored vegetable shortening, cubed

Instructions

For cookie mix: In each of 6 vacuum bags, Mylar bags, or jars, add and then seal:

- 2¼ cups rolled oats
- ¾ cups sugar
- ¾ cups flour
- ¾ cups M&Ms
- ¾ teaspoon salt
- ½ teaspoon baking soda
- 1 tablespoon dry milk
- 1 tablespoon powdered eggs
- ¼ teaspoon powdered vanilla

For shortening: In each of 6 vacuum bags, add and then seal:

- ¾ cup butter-flavored shortening, cubed

 Ready-Made Meal Assembly
In a Mylar bag, tote bag, or vacuum bag, store:

- 1 jar or pouch cookie mix
- 1 packet shortening

 Label each bag
To prepare, preheat the oven to 375°F. In a large bowl, combine the shortening, cookie mix, and ¼ cup of water and stir until a stiff dough forms. Drop rounded tablespoons onto a baking sheet about 2 inches apart. Bake for 10 to 12 minutes, until the edges are golden brown. Makes 4 dozen.

Sugar Cookies

Makes 6 batches (about 6 dozen cookies each)

Ingredients

3 cups powdered sugar

9 cups granulated sugar, divided

6 tablespoons powdered eggs

15 cups flour

3 teaspoons powdered vanilla

3 teaspoons baking soda

3 teaspoons cream of tartar

6 cups butter-flavored vegetable shortening

Instructions

For cookie mix, in each of 6 vacuum bags, Mylar bags, or jars, add and then seal:

- ½ cup powdered sugar
- ½ cup granulated sugar
- 1 tablespoon powdered eggs
- 2¼ cups flour
- ½ teaspoon powdered vanilla
- ½ teaspoon baking soda
- ½ teaspoon cream of tartar

For shortening: In each of 6 vacuum bags, add and then seal:

- 1 cup butter-flavored shortening

For extra sugar (for tops of cookies): In each of 6 vacuum bags, add and then seal:

- 1 cup sugar

 Ready-Made Meal Assembly

- 1 jar or pouch cookie mix
- 1 packet extra sugar
- 1 packet shortening

 Label each bag

Preheat oven to 375°F. In a large bowl, combine the shortening, cookie mix, and 2 tablespoons of water until a stiff dough forms. Drop by rounded tablespoons onto a baking sheet about 2 inches apart. Flatten with a glass dipped in sugar from the extra sugar packet. Bake for 7 to 9 minutes, until the edges are golden brown. Makes about 6 dozen.

Chocolate Chip Cookies

Makes 6 batches (about 4 dozen cookies each)

Ingredients

9 cups butter-flavored vegetable shortening

15 cups all-purpose flour

3 tablespoons baking soda

3 tablespoons salt

18 cups chocolate chips

9 cups brown sugar, packed

6 cups granulated sugar

¾ cup powdered eggs

1 tablespoon powdered vanilla

Instructions

For cookie mix: In each of 6 vacuum bags, add and then seal:

- 1½ cups shortening

For cookie mix: In each of 6 vacuum bags, Mylar bags, or jars, add and then seal:

- 2½ cups all-purpose flour
- 1½ teaspoons baking soda
- 1½ teaspoons salt
- 3 cups chocolate chips
- 1½ cups brown sugar, packed
- 1 cup granulated sugar
- 2 tablespoons powdered eggs
- ½ teaspoon powdered vanilla

 Ready-Made Meal Assembly

In a Mylar bag, tote bag, or vacuum bag, store:

- 1 jar or pouch cookie mix
- 1 packet shortening

Label each bag

Preheat the oven to 375°F. In a large bowl, combine the shortening, cookie mix, and ¼ cup of water until a stiff dough forms. Drop by rounded tablespoons onto a baking sheet about 2 inches apart. Bake for 10 to 12 minutes or until the edges are golden brown. Makes about 4 dozen.

Cranberry Walnut Oatmeal Cookies

Makes 6 batches (about 6 dozen cookies each)

Ingredients

4½ cups granulated sugar

4½ cups brown sugar, packed

¾ cup powdered eggs

6 cups flour

2 tablespoons powdered vanilla

2 tablespoons baking soda

2 tablespoons ground cinnamon

½ tablespoon salt

16½ cups rolled oats

6 cups dried cranberries

6 cups chopped walnuts

4½ cups butter-flavored vegetable shortening

Instructions

For cookie mix: In each of 6 vacuum bags, Mylar bags, or jars, add and then seal:

- ¾ cup granulated sugar
- ¾ cup brown sugar, packed
- 2 tablespoons powdered eggs
- 1 cup flour
- 1 teaspoon powdered vanilla
- 1 teaspoon baking soda
- 1 teaspoon ground cinnamon
- ¼ teaspoon salt

For oats, nuts, and dried cranberries: In each of 6 vacuum bags, add and then seal:

- 2¾ cups rolled oats
- 1 cup dried cranberries
- 1 cup chopped walnuts

For shortening: In each of 6 vacuum bags, add and then seal:

- ¾ cup butter-flavored shortening

 Ready-Made Meal Assembly

In a Mylar bag, tote bag, or vacuum bag, store:

- 1 jar or pouch cookie mix
- 1 packet oats, nuts, and dried cranberries
- 1 packet shortening

 Label each bag

Preheat the oven to 375°F. In a large bowl, combine the shortening, cookie mix, and ¼ cup of water until a stiff dough forms. Add the oats, nuts, and dried cranberries and stir to combine. Drop by rounded tablespoons onto a baking sheet about 2 inches apart. Bake for 10 to 12 minutes, or until edges are golden brown. Makes about 6 dozen.

Pecan Sandies

Makes 6 batches (about 3 dozen cookies each)

Ingredients

7½ cups powdered sugar, divided

12 cups flour

2 tablespoons powdered vanilla

6 cups chopped walnuts or pecans

6 cups butter-flavored vegetable shortening

Instructions

For cookie mix: In each of 6 vacuum bags, Mylar bags, or jars, add and then seal:

- ¼ cup powdered sugar
- 2 cups flour
- 1 teaspoon powdered vanilla
- 1 cup chopped walnuts or pecans

For extra sugar for rolling cookies: In each of 6 vacuum bags, add and then seal:

- 1 cup powdered sugar

For nuts: In each of 6 vacuum bags, add and then seal:

- 1 cup chopped walnuts or pecans

For shortening: In each of 6 vacuum bags, add and then seal:

- 1 cup shortening

 Ready-Made Meal Assembly
In a Mylar bag, tote bag, or vacuum bag, store:

- 1 jar or pouch cookie mix
- 1 packet nuts
- 1 packet extra sugar
- 1 packet shortening

Label each bag
Preheat the oven to 375°F. In a large bowl, combine the shortening, cookie mix, and 1 tablespoon of water until a stiff dough forms. Stir in the nuts. Roll the dough into small balls about the size of walnuts and place onto a baking sheet about 2 inches apart. Bake for 20 minutes or until lightly brown. Roll in extra powdered sugar to coat while still hot. Makes about 3 dozen.

Cowboy Cookies (Oatmeal Chocolate Chip)

Makes 6 batches (about 4 dozen cookies each)

Ingredients

6 cups butter-flavored vegetable shortening

6 cups granulated sugar

6 cups brown sugar, packed

¾ cup powdered eggs

2 tablespoons powdered vanilla

12 cups flour

3 tablespoons baking powder

3 teaspoons salt

12 cups chocolate chips

12 cups rolled oats

Instructions

For shortening: In each of 6 vacuum bags, add and then seal:

- 1 cup shortening

For cookie mix: In each of 6 vacuum bags, Mylar bags, or jars, add and then seal:

- 1 cup granulated sugar
- 1 cup brown sugar, packed
- 2 tablespoons powdered eggs
- 1 teaspoon powdered vanilla
- 2 cups flour
- 2 teaspoons baking powder
- ½ teaspoon salt

For chocolate chips and oats: In each of 6 vacuum bags, add and then seal:

- 2 cups chocolate chips
- 2 cups rolled oats

 Ready-Made Meal Assembly

In a Mylar bag, tote bag, or vacuum bag, store:

- 1 jar or pouch cookie mix
- 1 packet shortening
- 1 packet chocolate chips and oats

> **Label each bag**
> Preheat the oven to 350°F. In a large bowl, combine the shortening, cookie mix, and 2 tablespoons of water until a stiff dough forms. Drop by rounded tablespoons onto a baking sheet about 2 inches apart. Bake for 10 to 12 minutes, or until edges are golden brown. Makes about 4 dozen.

Peanut Butter Cookies

Makes 6 batches (about 3 dozen cookies each)

Ingredients

3 cups granulated sugar

3 cups brown sugar

6 tablespoons powdered eggs

7½ cups flour

4½ teaspoons baking soda

3 teaspoons baking powder

1½ teaspoons salt

3 cups peanut butter, chunky or creamy

3 cups butter-flavored vegetable shortening

Instructions

For cookie mix: In each of 6 vacuum bags, Mylar bags, or jars, add and then seal:

- ½ cup granulated sugar
- ½ cup brown sugar
- 1 tablespoon powdered eggs
- 1¼ cups flour
- ¾ teaspoons baking soda
- ½ teaspoon baking powder
- ¼ teaspoon salt

For peanut butter: In each of 6 vacuum bags or disposable 4-ounce containers, add and then seal:

- ½ cup (4 ounces) peanut butter

For shortening: In each of 6 vacuum bags, add and then seal:

- ½ cup shortening

 Ready-Made Meal Assembly
In a Mylar bag, tote bag, or vacuum bag, store:

- 1 jar or pouch cookie mix
- 1 packet peanut butter
- 1 packet shortening

> **Label**
> Preheat the oven to 375°F. In a large bowl, combine the shortening, cookie mix, and 2 tablespoons of water until a stiff dough forms. Roll into small balls about the size of walnuts and flatten with a fork in a crisscross pattern. Place on a baking sheet about 2 inches apart. Bake for 10 to 12 minutes or until lightly brown. Makes about 3 dozen.

White Chocolate Cranberry Cookies

Makes 6 batches (about 4 dozen cookies each)

Ingredients

9 cups butter-flavored vegetable shortening

15 cups flour

3 tablespoons baking soda

3 tablespoons salt

6 cups white chocolate chips

6 cups dried cranberries

9 cups brown sugar, packed

6 cups granulated sugar

¾ cup powdered eggs

1 tablespoon powdered vanilla

Instructions

For shortening: In each of 6 vacuum bags, add and then seal:

- 1½ cups shortening

For cookie mix: In each of 6 vacuum bags, Mylar bags, or jars add and then seal:

- 2½ cups flour
- 1½ teaspoons baking soda
- 1½ teaspoons salt
- 1½ cups white chocolate chips
- 1½ cups dried cranberries
- 1½ cups brown sugar, packed
- 1 cup granulated sugar
- 2 tablespoons powdered eggs
- ½ teaspoon powdered vanilla

Ready-Made Meal Assembly

In a Mylar bag, tote bag, or vacuum bag, store:

- 1 jar or pouch cookie mix
- 1 packet shortening

Label

Preheat the oven to 375°F. In a large bowl, combine the shortening, cookie mix, and ¼ cup of water until a stiff dough forms. Drop by rounded tablespoons onto a baking sheet about 2 inches apart. Bake for 10 to 12 minutes or until edges are golden brown. Makes about 4 dozen.

Butterscotch Cookies

Makes 6 batches (about 8 dozen cookies each)

Ingredients

9 cups butter-flavored vegetable shortening

18 cups brown sugar, packed

1¼ cups powdered eggs

2 tablespoons powdered vanilla

31½ cups flour

6 tablespoons baking powder

3 tablespoons baking soda

1 tablespoon cream of tartar

Instructions

For shortening: In each of 6 vacuum bags, add and then seal:

- 1½ cups shortening

For cookie mix: In each of 6 vacuum bags, Mylar bags, or jars, add and then seal:

- 3 cups brown sugar, packed
- 3 tablespoons powdered eggs
- 1 teaspoon powdered vanilla
- 5¼ cups flour
- 1 tablespoon baking powder
- 1½ teaspoons baking soda
- ½ teaspoon cream of tartar

Ready-Made Meal Assembly

In a Mylar bag, tote bag, or vacuum bag, store:

- 1 jar or pouch cookie mix
- 1 packet shortening

Label each bag

Preheat the oven to 350°F. In a large bowl, combine the shortening, cookie mix, and ¼ cup of water until a stiff dough forms. Drop by rounded tablespoons onto a baking sheet about 2 inches apart. Bake for 10 to 12 minutes or until edges are golden brown. Makes 8 dozen cookies.

Magic Bar Cookies

Magic bar cookies are called "magic" because they are assembled right in their baking dish in layers and no mixing is required. They are "transformed" right in the pan as the ingredients bake together. They are ooey, gooey, and delicious.

Makes 6 batches (for one 8 x 8-inch pan of 16 cookies each)

Ingredients

3 cups ghee

60 graham crackers, or 12 cups crushed

6 cups shredded or flaked coconut (sweetened or unsweetened)

6 cups chocolate chips

6 cups butterscotch chips (optional)

6 cups chopped almonds, walnuts, pecans, or a combination

6 (12-ounce) cans sweetened condensed milk

Instructions

For ghee: In each of 6 quarter-pint or 4-ounce jars, seal:

- ½ cup ghee

For graham crackers: In each of 6 vacuum bags add, and then seal

- 10 whole graham crackers or 1½ cups of crushed graham cracker crumbs

Note: Use a food processor to easily crush graham crackers into crumbs.

For chip, nut, and coconut mix: In each of 6 vacuum bags, Mylar bags, or jars, add and then seal:

- 1 cup shredded or flaked coconut, sweetened or not
- 1 cup chocolate chips
- 1 cup butterscotch chips (optional)
- 1 cup chopped almonds, walnuts, or pecans, or a combination

 Ready-Made Meal Assembly

In a Mylar bag, tote bag, or vacuum bag, store:

- 1 container ghee
- 1 packet graham crackers
- 1 packet nuts, chocolate chips, and coconut
- 1 can sweetened condensed milk

 Label each bag

Preheat the oven to 350°F. Melt the ghee and spread in an 8 x 8-inch baking pan. Crush the graham crackers into crumbs and layer evenly on top of the ghee. Add the chip, nut, and coconut mixture and spread evenly over the crumbs. Drizzle the condensed milk over the ingredients in the pan in an even layer. Bake for 30 to 35 minutes, until golden. Let cool and then cut into 2-inch squares. Makes 16.

Sugar and Spice Nuts

Makes 6 kits (about 3 cups each)

Ingredients

6 cups pecan halves

6 cups walnuts

6 cups cashews

6 cups sugar

4 tablespoons ground cinnamon

1 tablespoon ground cloves

1 tablespoon ground ginger

1 tablespoon ground nutmeg

1½ teaspoons powdered vanilla

2 tablespoons powdered egg whites

2 cups butter-flavored vegetable shortening or ghee, cubed

Instructions

For nuts: In each of 6 vacuum bags, Mylar bags, or jars, add and then seal:

- 1 cup pecan halves
- 1 cup walnuts
- 1 cup cashews

For sugar and spice mix: In each of 6 vacuum bags, Mylar bags, or jars add and then seal:

- 1 cup sugar
- 2 teaspoons ground cinnamon
- ½ teaspoon ground cloves
- ½ teaspoon ground ginger
- ½ teaspoon ground nutmeg
- ¼ teaspoon powdered vanilla

For eggs: In each of 6 vacuum bags, add and then seal:

- 2 tablespoons powdered egg whites

For shortening: In each of 6 vacuum bags, add and then seal:

- ⅓ cup shortening (cubes are easiest to measure and package) or ghee

 Ready-Made Meal Assembly

In a Mylar bag, tote bag, or vacuum bag, store:

- 1 packet shortening or ghee
- 1 packet egg whites
- 1 packet sugar and spice mix
- 1 packet nuts

 Label each bag

Preheat the oven to 350°F. Melt the ghee or shortening. In a large bowl, combine the powdered egg whites with 2 tablespoons of water and whisk until very foamy. Whisk in the sugar and spice packet. Whisk in the melted shortening or ghee and then add the nuts, stirring to coat thoroughly. Spread the nuts out on a rimmed baking sheet lined with foil or greased. Bake for 20 to 25 minutes, until golden, stirring periodically. Makes about 3 cups.

Chapter 11
Logistics

Storage Bags

Reusable tote bags are a great way to package your ready-made meals. Send a family member into the pantry to choose the meal of their choice and then prepare the meal as part of your family meal rotation and then use the bag again when you package up more meals. Alternatively, you can store your meal kits in Mylar bags. Mylar is very tough, lightweight, and flexible.

How to Stock Your Pantry

A good place to start is with sidekits. Plan to package large volumes of Rice (page 120), Mashed Potatoes (page 122), Polenta (page 121), and Buttered Noodles (page 120), because these sidekits will go with many recipes. Then when you package the beef or chicken with vegetables, you'll have a selection of sidekits ready to go.

After you've got a supply of sidekits, the next step is to stock your pantry with ready-made meals by focusing on one protein at a time—chicken, for example—and make several varieties of meals for that protein, and then move on to beef or pork. A good strategy is to go to a club or warehouse store and buy large quantities of what's on sale and make meals for that item.

It is also a good idea to schedule a day to make just breakfasts to store and a day to make lunches or desserts, etc.

Plan to invite a group of friends and divvy up the work while enjoying each other's company. Ask everyone to bring their pressure canners and vacuum-sealers. Organize the group into stations, each making a recipe or set of recipes, or have one team do all the vacuum-sealing, one group all the labeling, etc.

Buying in Bulk

Amazon.com has a feature called "Subscribe and Save," which allows you to buy items at a discount and is really good for items that are not carried at your local grocery store. For example, my local grocery store doesn't carry butter-flavored shortening in cubes, which are SO easy to cut into measured chunks and vacuum-seal. With Subscribe and Save, you sign up to receive something on a specific interval of your choosing, and then you get a discount on the item. I also use this for pint-size cans of spaghetti sauce, which is more economical in my area than buying tomatoes.

Another great idea is to go to your local agricultural area in the summer and buy large quantities of fruit from the farmers to can and dehydrate, giving you more ingredients to add to your shelf-stable pantry.

Bug-Out Bins

A bug-out bin is a container that holds enough supplies for your family to survive for several days away from home in an emergency. They're popular because many people who choose to store shelf-stable food also envision scenarios in which they might have to leave their house quickly, such as due to a flood or fire. For such situations, it's a great idea to package meals into plastic bins each containing a week or 10 days' worth of food. Plan to include breakfasts, lunches, dinners, snacks, treats, and beverages, and make sure you also have a box of portable cooking equipment, including:

Checklist of Portable Kitchen Equipment

- ❏ Skillet
- ❏ Soup pot
- ❏ Large and small saucepans
- ❏ Lids to fit pots
- ❏ Spatulas, spoons, silverware, chef's knives
- ❏ Cutting boards
- ❏ Strainer
- ❏ Food mill
- ❏ Can opener
- ❏ Measuring cups
- ❏ Bowls
- ❏ Portable barbecue grill with briquettes or other fuel

Conversions

MEASURE	EQUIVALENT	METRIC
1 teaspoon	--	5.0 milliliters
1 tablespoon	3 teaspoons	14.8 milliliters
1 cup	16 tablespoons	236.8 milliliters
1 pint	2 cups	473.2 milliliters
1 quart	4 cups	946.4 milliliters
1 gallon	4 quarts (16 cups)	3.785 liters
1 liter	4 cups + 3½ tablespoons	1000 milliliters
1 ounce (dry)	2 tablespoons	28.35 grams
1 pound	16 ounces	453.49 grams
2.21 pounds	35.3 ounces	1 kilogram
5 pounds flour	about 18 cups	2.27 kilograms
120°F / 350°F / 375°F / 450°F	--	49°C / 177°C / 190°C / 232°C

Recipe Index

Acknowledgments

I would like to thank Lynnette Wineman, who set me on this course, my husband for his unfailing support, and my many recipe tasters and testers. I am also grateful to Kelly Reed, my editor, Kim Nelson my very gifted photographer, and all those who helped in the design and editing of this book. Thank you for your support and encouragement, and for your many talents.

About the Author

Julie Languille is passionate about both food and preparedness. She owns a dinner-planning website with thousands of recipes compiled to make dinner planning, shopping, and cooking easy for families. She teaches workshops on preparedness and long-term food storage, and regularly hosts food-packaging parties where families gather to make prepackaged meal kits to build their own food storage as well as bless families in need. Julie lives with her husband and family on lovely Whidbey Island, in the Puget Sound near Seattle, and when not cooking she loves to read, sail, and kayak in the waters near her home.